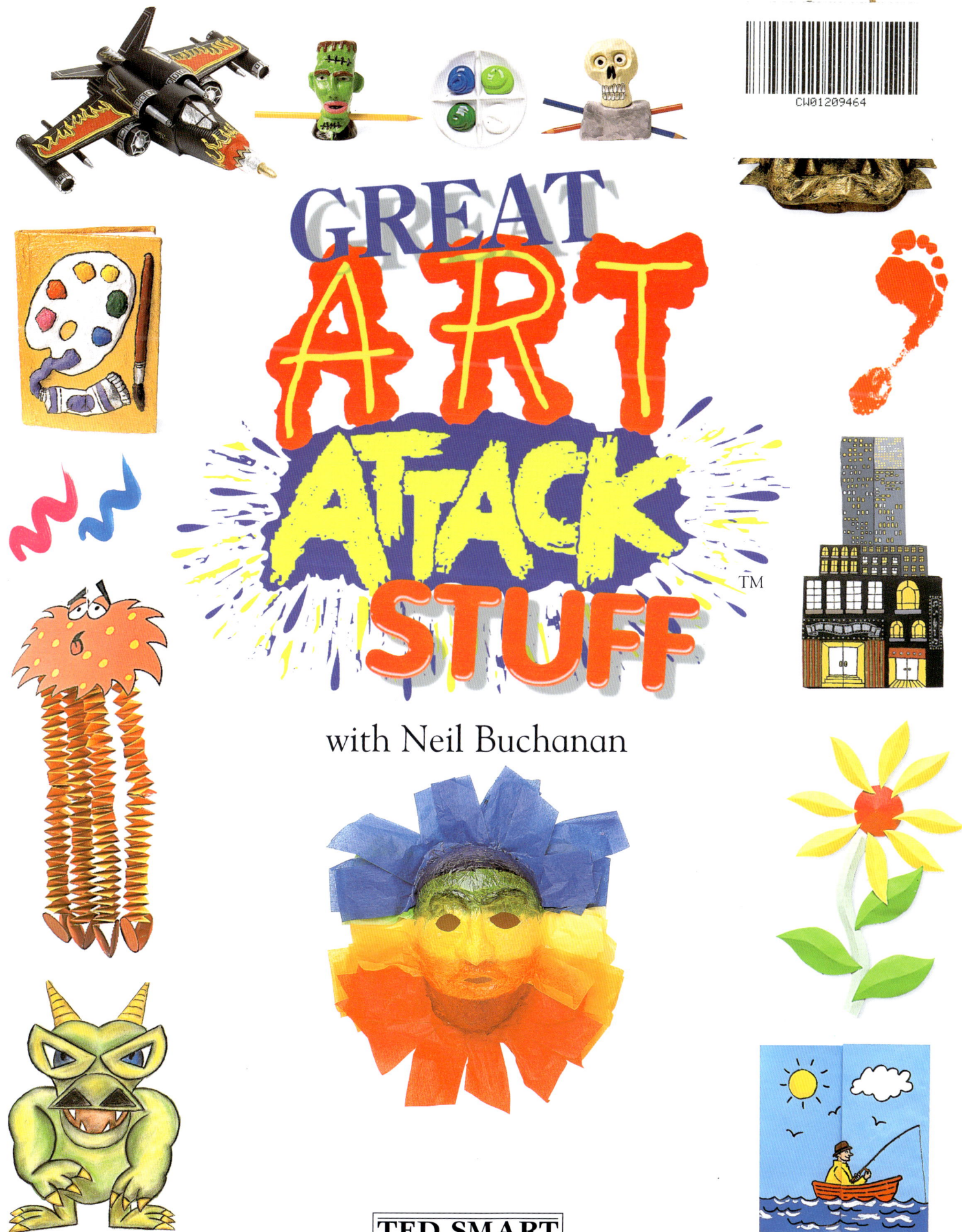

ART ATTACK

LONDON, NEW YORK, MELBOURNE,
MUNICH and DELHI

Designer Jacqueline Gooden
Editor Penelope York
Senior Art Editor Rebecca Johns
Senior Editor Fiona Robertson

Prop Maker Jim Copley
Photographer Steve Gorton

Managing Art Editor Rachael Foster
Managing Editor Mary Ling
Production Lisa Moss
DTP Designer Almudena Díaz

First published in Great Britain in 1999 by
Dorling Kindersley Limited, 80 Strand, London WC2R 0RL

2 4 6 8 10 9 7 5 3 1

Copyright © 2006 Dorling Kindersley Limited, London

This edition produced for The Book People Ltd,
Hall Wood Avenue, Haydock, St Helens WA11 9UL

All rights reserved. No part of this publication may be reproduced, stored in a retrieval system, or transmitted in any form or by any means, electronic, mechanical, photocopying, recording, or otherwise, without the prior written permission of the copyright owner.

A CIP catalogue record for this book
is available from the British Library.

ISBN: 1-4053-1825-2
ISBN: 978-1-4053-1825-9

Colour reproduction by MDP, UK
Printed and bound by Toppan Printing, China

Dorling Kindersley would like to thank everyone at
Media Merchants for their help and enthusiasm.

Additional thanks to Gill Cooling for editorial help, Piers Tilbury for
jacket design and Gary Ombler for additional photography.

CONTENTS

INTRODUCTION 4–5
WACKY WATCH 6–7

COOL CALENDAR 8–9
JUNGLE FRAME 10–11

WIGGLY EARS 12–13

WRITE AWAY 14–15
COLOUR WISE 16–17

FANTASY FLYER 18–19
ON A MISSION 20–21

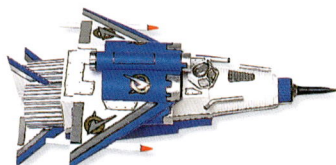 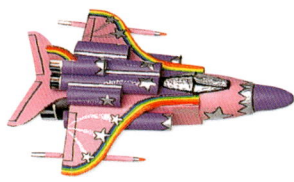

CRAZY COVERS 22–23
CHALKY FACE 24–25

CONTENTS

TOP T-SHIRTS 26–27
NEAR AND FAR 28–29

POP-UP CARD 30–31
PEN PAL 32–33

MAGIC MASK 34–35

FLOWER POWER 36–37
GLITTER FUN 38–39

LIGHT AND DARK 40–41
CREASED ART 42–43

3-D SCENE 44–45
IN THE FRAME 46–47

IN A FLAP 48–49
ON THE EDGE 50–51

GRIM GARGOYLE 52–53

SWINGY SPIDER 54–55

COLOUR WAVES 56–57

VIDEO CITY 58–59
CITY LIGHTS 60–61

HANDY TIPS 62–63
INDEX 64

ART ATTACK ★ *Remember to get permission before you start any of the projects in Art Attack Great Stuff.*

INTRODUCTION

Hi! It's great to be back with Art Attack Great Stuff – another collection of ideas that are easy to make, look great, and have wonderful uses! This book is not only filled with fantastic 3-D models and top decorations – you can also learn how to create really fabulous pictures using some amazing techniques! Have fun and remember that you don't have to be good at art to create amazing Art Attacks! Try them yourself – collect some bits and pieces, grab your pencils and paints, and have an Art Attack!

Neil Buchanan

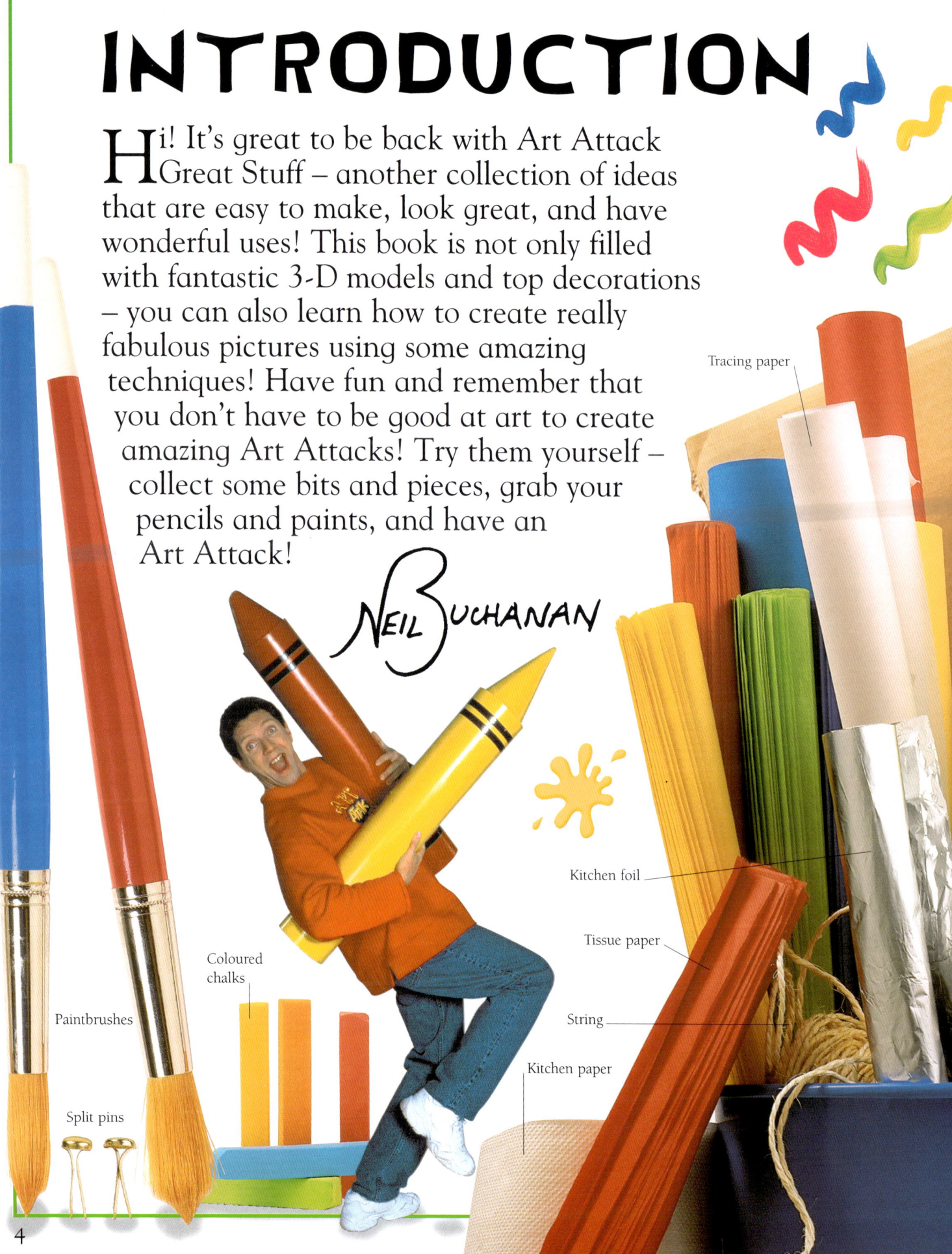

ART ATTACK

WACKY WATCH

Are you always forgetting what day of the month it is? This big watch calendar could be the answer – not to tell you the time, but the date!

From card to calendar

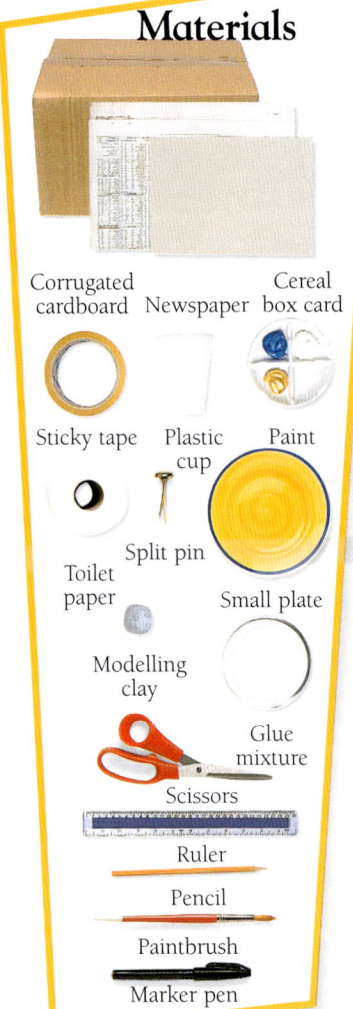

Materials

Corrugated cardboard
Newspaper
Cereal box card
Sticky tape
Plastic cup
Paint
Split pin
Toilet paper
Small plate
Modelling clay
Glue mixture
Scissors
Ruler
Pencil
Paintbrush
Marker pen

Place a ball of modelling clay behind the card to push your pencil into.

1 Using the side from a cardboard box, draw around a small plate onto the card. Accurately mark the centre of the circle using a ruler.

2 Cut the circle out and make a hole in the centre by pushing a pencil through the point you've marked. This is your big watch face.

Make sure you roll the newspaper up tightly.

Scrunch up a small ball of newspaper and place it on the side of the watch as a winder.

Roll up a small piece of paper and lay it across the middle of the loop to form the pin. Tape it into place.

5 Turn the watch over and give it a chunky, 3-D effect using newspaper. Roll up a sausage of newspaper and give it a twist to keep it in place. Wrap it around the outside of the watch face and tape it into place.

6 To make the buckle, take a smaller piece of newspaper and roll it up into a sausage shape. Bend the scrunched-up paper into a C-shape and tape it to the straight end of the watchstrap in a loop.

WACKY WATCH

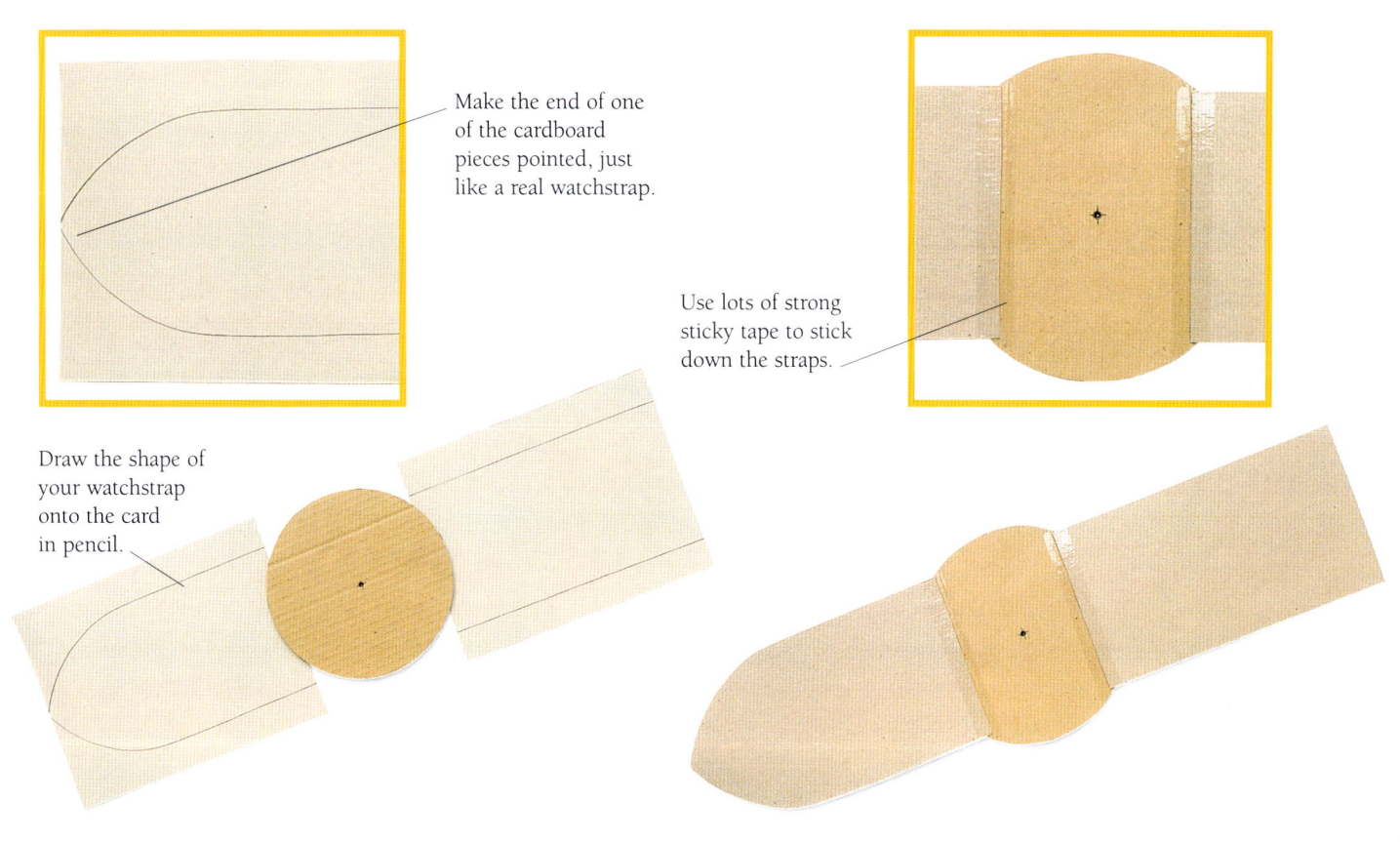

Make the end of one of the cardboard pieces pointed, just like a real watchstrap.

Use lots of strong sticky tape to stick down the straps.

Draw the shape of your watchstrap onto the card in pencil.

3 For the watchstrap cut the front and back off a cereal box and place them either side of the watch face. Draw a watchstrap that is slightly narrower than the watch face. Cut out the two parts of the strap.

4 Overlap the straps onto the edge of the cut-out cardboard circle and fix them into place. This will form the back of your watch, so make sure that the straps are securely fixed.

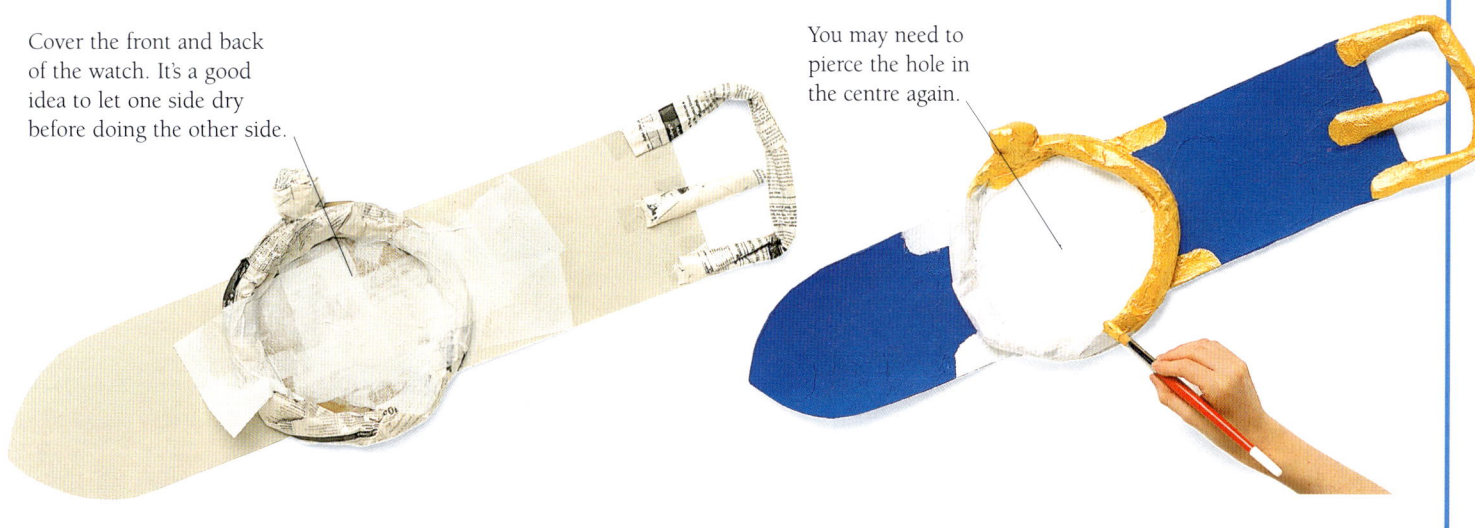

Cover the front and back of the watch. It's a good idea to let one side dry before doing the other side.

You may need to pierce the hole in the centre again.

7 To make your basic watch shape really strong, cover it with the glue mixture and then stick toilet paper onto the pasted areas. Leave to dry overnight and the glue will turn hard and strong.

8 Use acrylic or poster paint to decorate your watch. Paint the face white and the strap a bright colour to make it look like plastic. Paint the metal parts gold so that they look really smart.

ART ATTACK

COOL CALENDAR

A few finishing touches and your calendar will be ready to use. Put it where you can see it easily and you'll never be stuck for the date again!

Helping hand
Watch that you don't make the hands too long, you don't want to cover the dates up completely!

The big hand must be long enough to reach the numbers on the outside of the face.

The small hand should reach the small numbers.

Try out your own strap designs, such as these brightly coloured polka dots.

Making the clock hands
Cut out two stiff cardboard hands and pierce a hole in the end of each one. Fix them to the middle of the watch face using a split pin. Open out the pin behind the watch.

The big numbers represent each month of the year.

When you are happy with the position of all the numbers, go over them in black marker pen.

Paint the watch hands to match the rest of the watch.

Paint the strap any colour and pattern you like. Finish it off by adding details, such as stitching, in black marker pen.

8

COOL CALENDAR

You can alter the date of any day of the year by moving the large hand to one of the 12 large numbers (the months), and the small hand to one of the 31 small numbers (the days).

Dotty dates
Try experimenting with lots of different colours and patterns for your calendar. You could even make a separate calendar for each of the main rooms in your house, so you always know the date!

Finishing your calendar
Once you've painted your big watch calendar, you can add lots of extra details to make it truly unique and ensure that none of your friends will have anything like it!

Draw around a plastic cup in the middle of the watch face to create a circle for the days.

Number crunching
When drawing the big numbers, start with the 12, 3, 6, and 9, and then neatly fill in the other numbers.

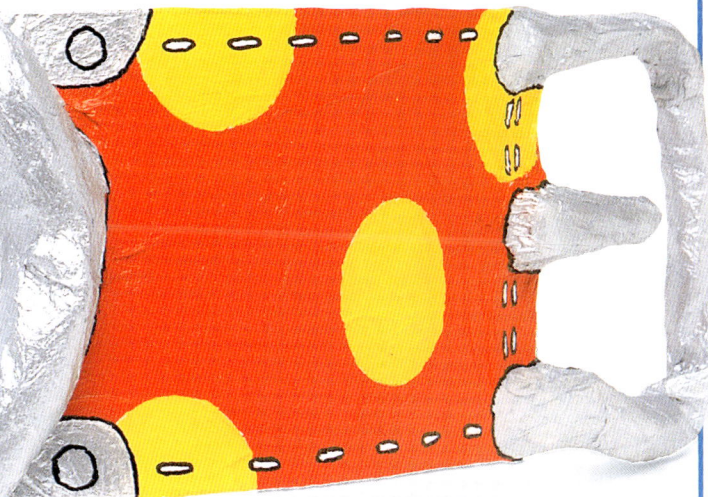

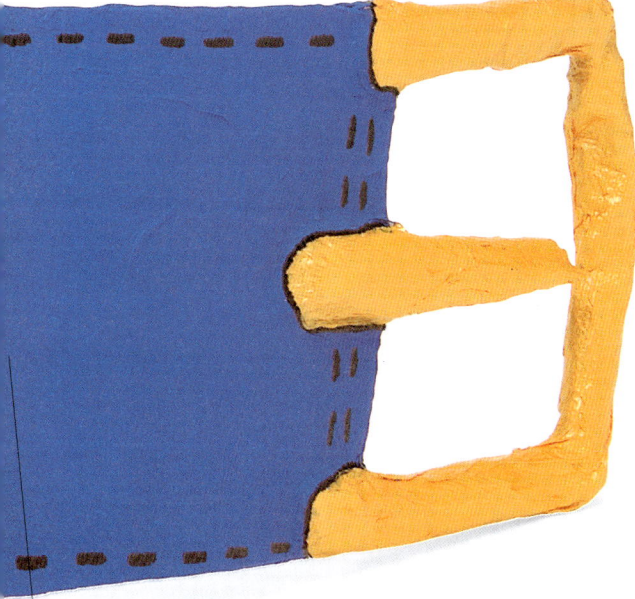

Bend the watchstrap backwards so you can stand it up on a tabletop.

Numbering the clock face
Your watch face has two circles with numbers on: 1–12 for the months and 1–31 for the days. The numbers should be evenly spaced. For the days, divide up the circle into 31 equally spaced sections.

9

ART ATTACK

JUNGLE FRAME

Have you got a picture or a photo that you'd like to frame in an unusual way? Why not give it a safari feel with one of these frames?

From sticks to frame

Make the frame twice the height and width of your picture.

Tie the loose ends together and trim them neatly.

Materials

- Newspaper and picture
- 2 long and 2 short sticks
- Kitchen roll
- Glue mixture
- String
- Glue stick
- Modelling clay
- Paint
- Scissors
- Paintbrush
- Pencil
- Marker pen

1 Take four chunky sticks and arrange them into a rectangular frame. Make sure that the sticks overlap each other in each of the four corners.

2 Cut a long piece of coarse string for each corner and use it to tie the sticks together. Wrap the string three times in one direction and then three times in the other.

The kitchen roll will create a ragged effect.

Paste on lots of layers to make it really thick.

Both sides can be used to display a picture, so don't forget to paint the back, too!

What a mess! Make sure you lay lots of newspaper down on your surface before you start pasting on the kitchen roll, it can be a messy business!

3 To make the crinkled leather backing, tear a piece of newspaper to fit in the frame. Paste the newspaper with the glue mixture and then cover it with lots of squares of kitchen roll.

4 Leave the glue to dry overnight into a stiff, crinkled "leather" effect. Use a tan-coloured poster or acrylic paint to paint both sides of the backing.

JUNGLE FRAME

Make sure each piece of string is long enough to reach the frame.

Use just a little glue around the edges of your picture.

5 Place a ball of modelling clay behind each corner and push a sharp pencil through the paper to make a hole. Thread a piece of string through each hole and then tie the string to each corner of the frame. Use the same string as you used to bind the corners.

6 Choose a picture or a photograph that will fit inside your frame. You may want to stick to the safari theme and find a picture of a fierce animal! Cut it out, put a few dabs of glue on the back, and position it in the middle.

Jungle safari frame
If you tie some string to the top stick, you can put your frame wherever you like – on a door handle, on a shelf, or even above your bed!

You can make your frame any size you like, depending on what you want to go in it.

Draw on extra details, such as footprints with a black marker pen.

Keep out!
If you haven't got a picture or a photo that you want to frame, why not make a safari sign for your bedroom?

ART ATTACK

WIGGLY EARS

Try this cheeky idea for size – a face with ears that wiggle, thanks to some card and some split pins!

From card to face

Materials

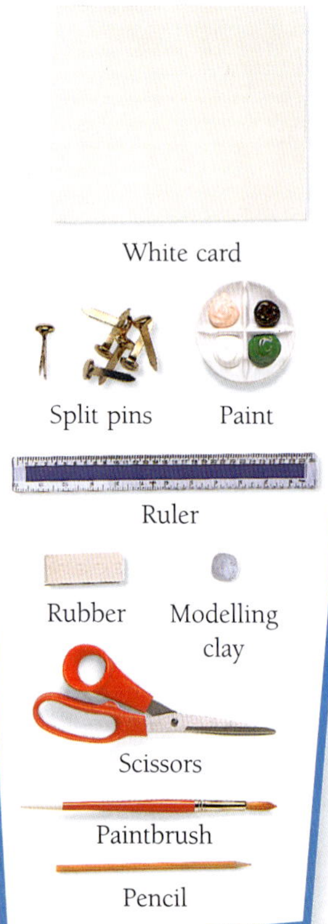

- White card
- Split pins
- Paint
- Ruler
- Rubber
- Modelling clay
- Scissors
- Paintbrush
- Pencil

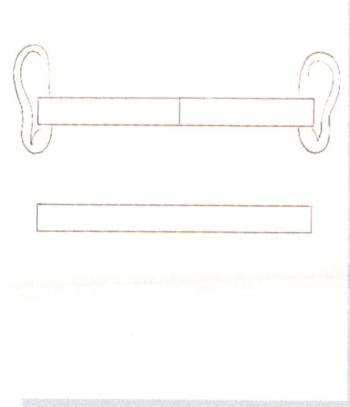

Place a lump of modelling clay behind the strip and make a hole by pushing a pencil point into it.

1 On a piece of card, draw around a 30-cm ruler twice. Draw an ear shape at each end of one of the strips. Cut out both strips, and cut the ear strip in half.

2 Pierce a hole 2 cm in from the end of the long strip, using modelling clay, as above. Make a hole at the ends of both ear strips, also 2 cm in.

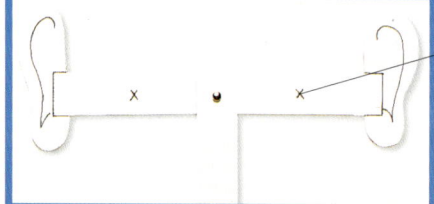

Mark a point midway between each ear and the split pin and make a hole through the marks.

These holes will be the eyes on your face. You will eventually attach your wiggly ears to the face through these holes.

3 Overlap the three pieces of card and join them together with a split pin. Fold back the edges of the pin to secure it. This is your wiggling ear mechanism.

4 Take another piece of thin card and place the wiggling ear mechanism on top. Mark on the card the position of the inside edges of the ears and the halfway holes on the ear strips.

Walter Wiggle Ears

When you have finished painting your face, cut it out. Place it on top of your wiggly ear mechanism and attach them together with split pins through the eyes, splitting the pin at the back. Turn Walter over and give him a good old wiggle!

Remember to paint the ears thoroughly to make sure you can see paint however hard you wiggle!

You can make the ears any shape you want – the weirder they are, the more effective the wiggle!

Make the features on your face really big to make your face more cartoon-like.

Pull this strip up and down to make the ears wiggle.

You can have endless fun with the wiggly ears! Try making monster faces as well.

Alien abduction
Paint a face bright green and surprise your friends with this spooky, wiggly-eared alien!

5 The idea is to draw a head that will fit within the wiggly ears. Use the two position dots as the centre of the eyes, and use a pencil point to push holes through them.

6 Once you are happy with your face it is ready to colour. Use acrylic or poster paints and remember to paint the ears too! Allow it to dry overnight.

ART ATTACK

WRITE AWAY

Personalized stationery can be expensive, so why not have some fun printing your own original designs – using your hands and feet!

From paper to personal stationery

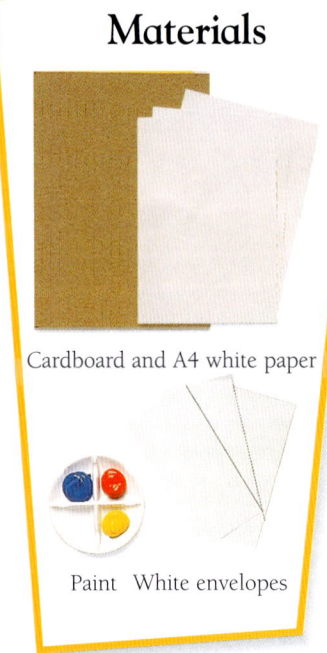

Materials

Cardboard and A4 white paper

Paint   White envelopes

Messy Business! Make sure you ask permission before you start. It's great fun but can be very messy! Try printing outside.

1 Place a piece of paper on newspaper. Dip your foot into some poster paint, and then press your foot on to the paper.

2 Experiment with the patterns you make on the paper. Try dipping your foot into lots of different coloured paint.

Put a couple of thumb prints on the envelope too, for an unusual effect.

Cut shaped templates out of cardboard.

3 Make some envelopes to match your writing paper! Follow the instructions above, but this time dip your hand in the paint, then press all or part of it firmly on the envelope.

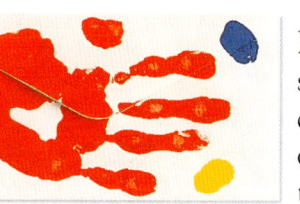

4 You can also use cardboard templates to decorate your stationery. Dip the template into some paint and press it down on to the paper or envelope for a nice textured finish.

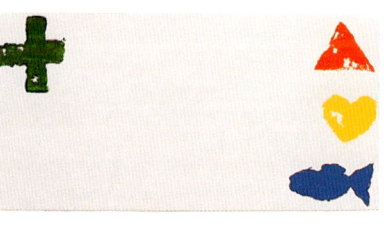

WRITE AWAY

Put your foot in it!

Now that you have decorated your paper, you are ready to sit down and write some letters! You could write to a relative, perhaps, to tell them about your weekend. Or maybe a close friend has moved and you want to catch up with their news.

Orchard Cottage
Little Hampton
Gloucestershire
GL8 2PY

1 April 1999

Dear Grandma and Grandpa

I hope you are well. I had a lovely time in Cornwall last weekend. The weather was very sunny and we spent lots of time playing on the beach. I built the biggest sandcastle of all!

The sea was very cold but we still swam all day. Jack has learnt to swim but he still has to wear arm bands when the waves are big.

Lots of love,

Emma

For a more interesting pattern, press only part of your foot on the paper and use lots of different colours.

Mr and Mrs H G Foote
The Gallery House
Art Attack Road
Maidstone
Kent TN20 9JY

Remember to address your letter correctly.

Clean fingers

Place a loop of tape on the back of the cardboard templates. You can use this to pick up a template and dip it in the paint without getting your fingers messy.

Up, up, and away!

Here's a clever idea – why not turn your thumb prints into balloons? Position the balloons on the page, as if they are floating, and draw pieces of string below them.

Decorate the envelopes to match the paper.

15

ART ATTACK

COLOUR WISE

Have you ever noticed how some colours give a warm feeling to your pictures and others give a cool feeling? Try drawing a picture using both.

A winter scene

Black paper

Coloured chalk

White chalk

Colour swatches
A good way to sort out your colours is to make a colour swatch for each season. Think of the appropriate colours and then draw them all on one sheet of paper as a guide.

This colour swatch has cool colours on the top half and warm colours on the bottom.

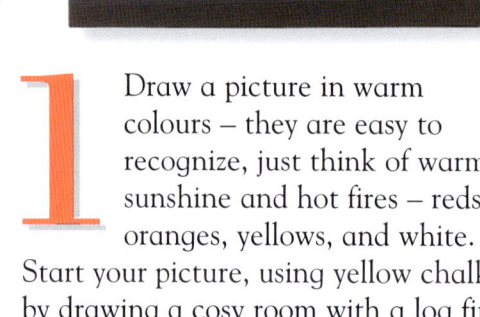

1 Draw a picture in warm colours – they are easy to recognize, just think of warm sunshine and hot fires – reds, oranges, yellows, and white. Start your picture, using yellow chalk, by drawing a cosy room with a log fire.

2 Bring some oranges and whites into the picture. The colours will help the fire glow with heat in the grate, and make the room feel cosier. Smudge the fire a little with your finger to spread the heat into the room.

3 To finish the warm colours, add some rich, hot reds. Highlight the fire with small strokes of red and draw in the curtains, chair, and lamp. Can you see how much warmer the room is by using these colours?

4 Finally put in the cool colours – snowy whites, icy blues, and minty greens. Put the colours in the window to make the outside seem snowy and cold. Now you can really see the difference between the warm and cool colours.

COLOUR WISE

Winter warmth
Even though you have used a black background, you still get a strong feeling of warmth just by using the right colours. The icy cool colours and the fiery hot colours really give the picture a cosy, wintery look.

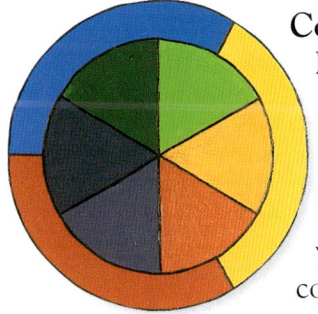

Colour wheel
Red, yellow, and blue are the primary colours. By mixing these colours correctly you can create any colour you want.

The winter colours give a frosty feeling to the outside world.

Autumn days
When you draw an autumn scene, imagine the colours of the falling leaves during this season – rich reds, oranges, and lots of browns. Draw your own autumnal picture using these colours.

Lazy summer
Try out the summer colours and think of strong yellow sunlight, which makes the colours bright and cheerful. Use the primary colours to help the picture seem really sunny.

Spring fever
Spring colours include blossom pinks, daffodil yellows, clear sky-blues, and fresh greens. Draw a picture with these colours and create a crisp, spring feeling.

17

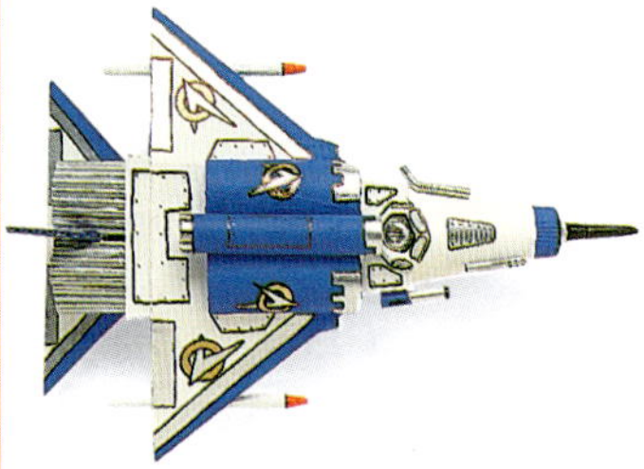

ART ATTACK

FANTASY FLYER

The fantastic futuristic fliers in computer games or space movies begin as models. Why not let your imagination run wild and design one yourself!

Materials

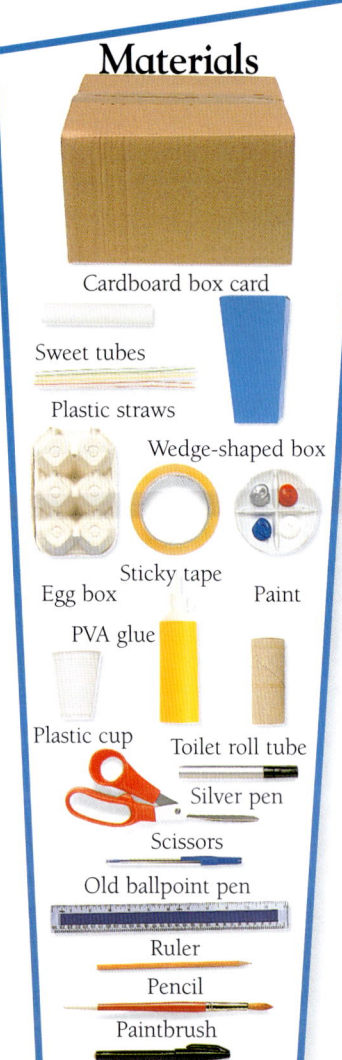

Cardboard box card
Sweet tubes
Plastic straws
Wedge-shaped box
Egg box
Sticky tape
Paint
PVA glue
Plastic cup
Toilet roll tube
Silver pen
Scissors
Old ballpoint pen
Ruler
Pencil
Paintbrush
Marker pen

From box to flyer

1 Take a wedge-shaped box and place it on to a strong piece of card. Draw a large, chunky, triangular wing on either side of the box.

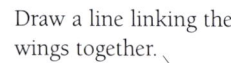
Draw a line linking the wings together.

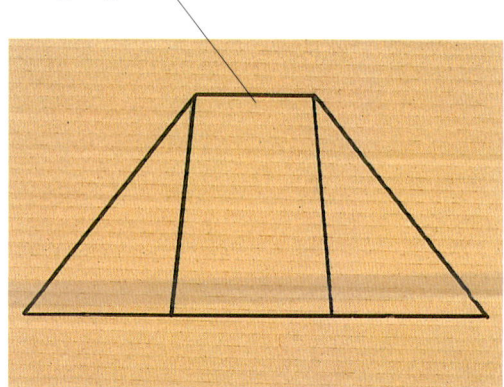

2 Remove the box and draw a line between the wings. Cut out the wings neatly, making them nice and straight. Take a ruler and use it to bend the wings (right).

Cut another toilet roll in to two halves and stick it on the underside of the plane, to match the one on top.

Stick a bottle top onto the cup at the front of the aircraft, and an old ball point pen lid onto this to make the aircraft streamlined.

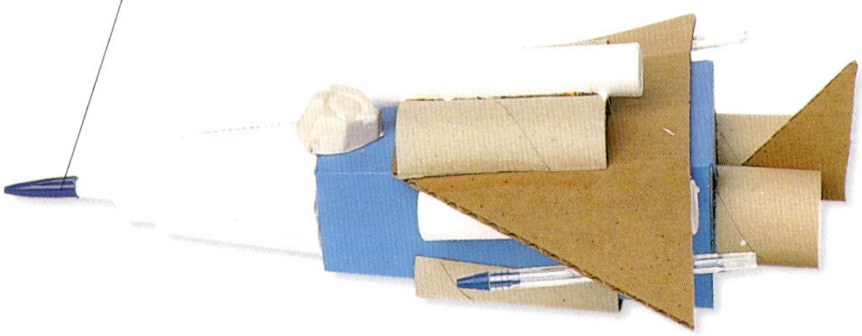

Stick a sweet tube between the two toilet roll halves on the top of the plane.

5 Cut down the length of a toilet roll and open it out so that you have two half circles, joined in the middle. Stick it to the top of the flyer to make it look hi-tech!

6 Stick sweet tubes and old ballpoint pens under the wings as jet engines and rockets. Put part of an egg box on the top of the plane as the cockpit.

FANTASY FLYER

Use a ruler to bend the edge of each wing along the line where it will overhang the body of the aircraft.

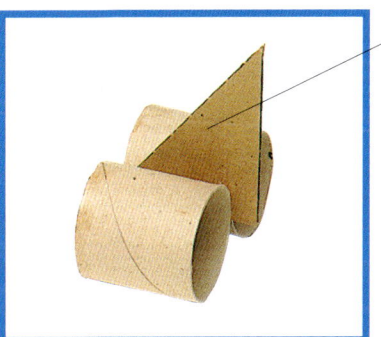

To form tail jets and a tail, cut a toilet roll in half and stick a triangle of cardboard in-between the two pieces using PVA glue.

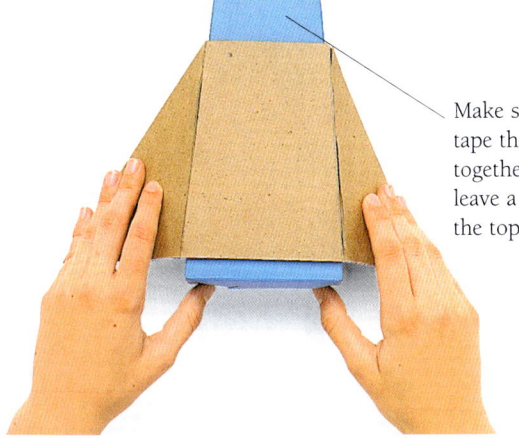

Make sure you tape the pieces together well and leave a space at the top of the box.

These main parts make up the basic structure, but to turn it into a fantasy fighter you need lots of cardboard and plastic tubes to stick all over the body.

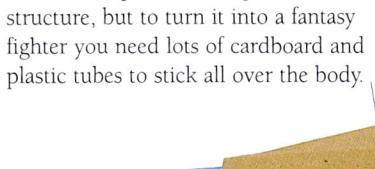

3 Turn the card over and place the wings over the wedge-shaped box, so that they slope downwards. Use sticky tape to fix them in position.

4 Stick a plastic cup to the front of the box to form the nose, and stick the tail and tail jets to the back. Take your time doing this; use lots of strong tape and be as neat as possible.

Cut a triangle of cardboard and stick it below the tail jets at the back of the plane to form the tail wings.

You can design and paint your plane any way you like, so that it really is your very own fantasy flyer!

7 Cut drinking straws and place them all over the toilet rolls at the tail end of the plane. Make sure all the pieces of the plane are firmly stuck before you begin to paint the flyer.

8 Your plane is now ready to paint. Use a silver pen to colour the jets and windows and acrylic or poster paint for the rest. Add some PVA glue to the poster paint to make it stick to the plastic parts of the plane.

ART ATTACK

ON A MISSION

Your flyers are now ready to go into battle! Hang them at different angles so they look as if they're zooming all around the room.

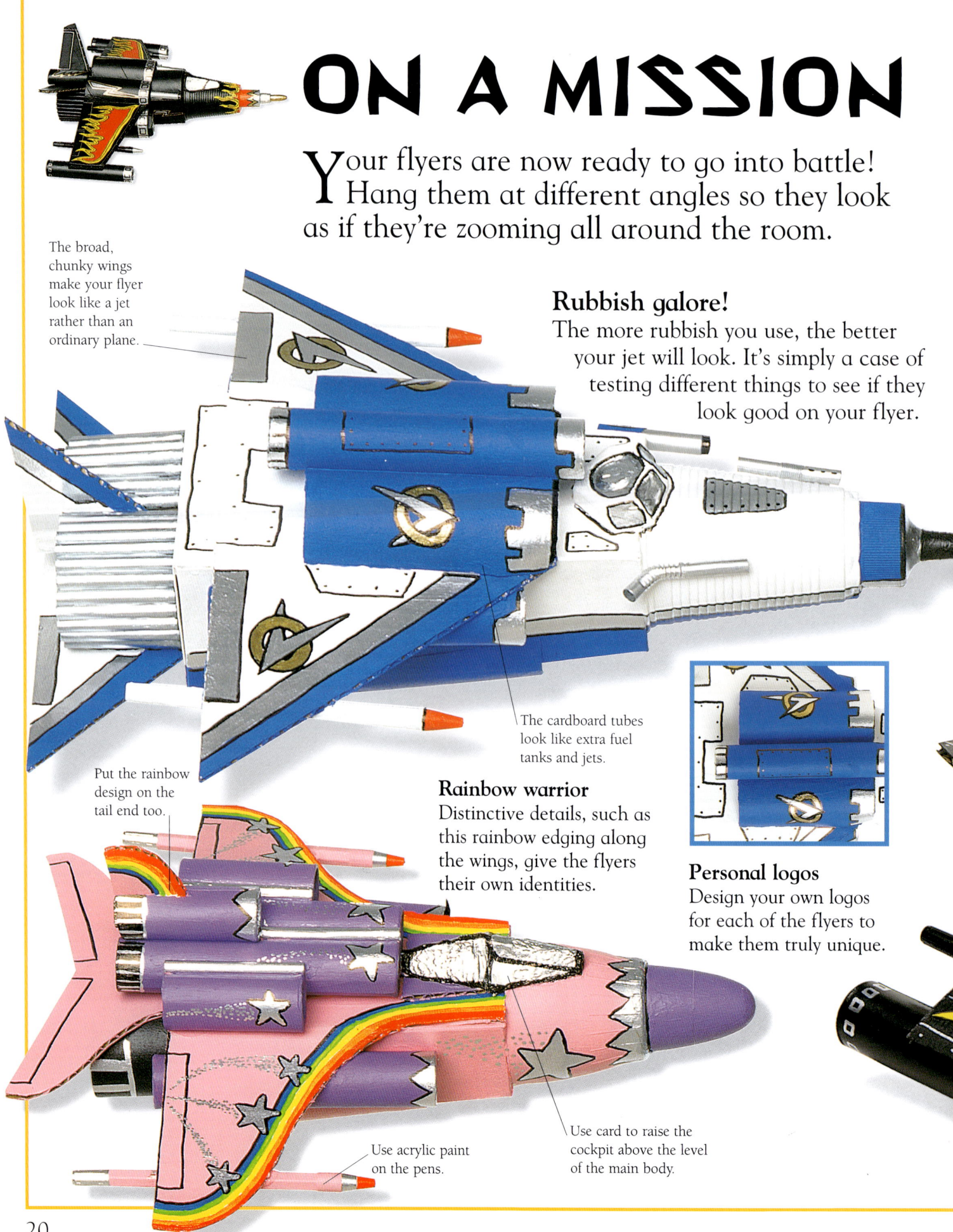

The broad, chunky wings make your flyer look like a jet rather than an ordinary plane.

Rubbish galore!
The more rubbish you use, the better your jet will look. It's simply a case of testing different things to see if they look good on your flyer.

The cardboard tubes look like extra fuel tanks and jets.

Rainbow warrior
Distinctive details, such as this rainbow edging along the wings, give the flyers their own identities.

Put the rainbow design on the tail end too.

Personal logos
Design your own logos for each of the flyers to make them truly unique.

Use acrylic paint on the pens.

Use card to raise the cockpit above the level of the main body.

ON A MISSION

Let battle commence!
Once you've made several flyers, you can send them into battle. Will they fight against each other, or will they unite to fight an unknown alien force?

Allow each layer of paint to dry before adding more.

Demon fighter
Remember that you're the designer and you can paint your flyer any colour you like. The more detail you add, the more it will look as if it's come straight out of the latest sci-fi movie.

Flaming fuel jets
Use red and orange paint inside the jets at the back to create flames.

The fiery flames on this flyer make it look as though it's roaring through the skies.

Don't throw away your old felt-tip pen lids – they look great as a streamlined tip for the flyer's nose!

Draw on extra details with marker pens when you've finished painting.

Boxed in
The wedge-shaped box is the initial shape of the flyer. Just add any old bits and pieces on to it that you choose!

Gold and silver pens give the flyer a great metallic look.

21

ART ATTACK

CRAZY COVERS

Are you fascinated by wonderful old books? Why not transform one of your own boring exercise books into an ancient personal diary!

From new book to old diary

Materials

Writing book and cloth
Toilet paper   Glue mixture
Shoe polish   Paint
Pencil
Paintbrush
Marker pen

Add as many layers of toilet paper as it takes to cover the book.

1 Take a plain exercise or hardback writing book and lay strips of toilet paper on the cover. Paint over the strips with the glue mixture. The toilet paper will stick to the book as it soaks up all the glue.

2 Cover the whole of the front and back of your book. It's also a good idea to coat the inside of the cover too, as this will help to stop the book warping outwards as it dries. Leave your book to dry overnight.

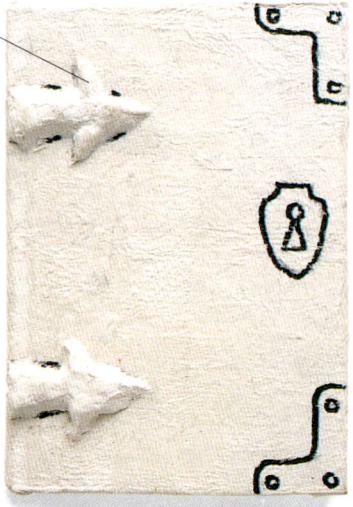

Simply press the pulp onto the book and mould it into shape with your fingers.

3 Your book is now ready to decorate. To make it look old, draw fancy hinges on the sides and metal ends with nails at the corners. Let others know it's a private diary by putting a lock and keyhole on it!

4 When your design is done, take some more strips of toilet paper and dip them into the glue mixture. Squeeze out the excess glue and use this pulp to build up your design into a 3-D relief. Leave it to dry overnight.

CRAZY COVERS

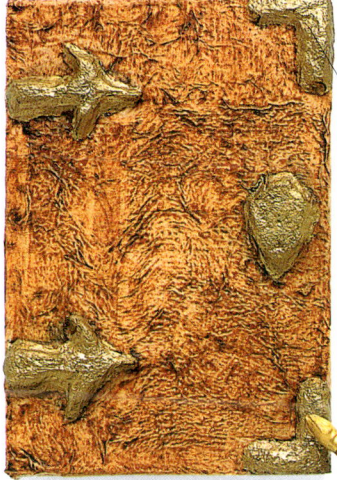

Use a soft cloth to rub the shoe polish into all the cracks and creases.

Use gold paint to create the metal effect.

5 Your cover is now ready to colour. You can use acrylic or poster paint, or even rub in some brown shoe polish for an "old leather" effect.

6 To finish off, colour the keyhole, hinges, and nails with gold paint. Draw around the edges of them with a black marker pen.

An ancient record
Your own ancient personal diary is the perfect place to record all your secrets. And the lock and keyhole warn others to stay out!

Use the pulp mixture to highlight some of the features on your cover.

Paint the inside of the keyhole black to make it look real.

Add details such as nail heads for a truly "old" effect.

Pretty palette
Try different looks for some of your other books, such as this bold and colourful palette for your sketch pad.

ART ATTACK

CHALKY FACE

Create your own crazy Art Attack face using a geometry set and some chalk pastels. Use all the shapes in the set for really wacky results!

From chalk to face

Materials
- White paper
- Geometry set
- Rubber
- Cotton wool
- Coloured chalk
- Black chalk
- Pencil

1 Draw around the shapes in a geometry set to create a face. There are lots of different shapes you can make by placing them at different angles.

Draw around the inside of a protractor for a smaller curve and the outside for a larger curve.

2 When you're happy with your design, use different coloured chalk or pastels to trace over the lines thickly. Blow off the excess dust.

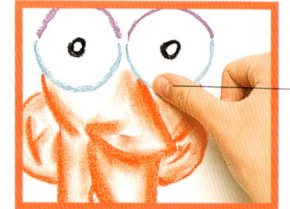

Use your thumb or finger to smudge the dust towards the centre of each section.

If you prefer, you can use your fingers instead of the cotton wool ball for this stage.

Use as many different colours as you want.

3 Smudge the chalk inwards with your fingertips. Go over the outline again with a pastel in a darker shade. Smudge this line as well to give your picture a dusty, smoky effect.

4 Go over each line with black chalk and lightly smudge it. Then dab a ball of cotton wool onto some of the excess coloured chalk dust, and dab this around the outside edge of the picture.

CHALKY FACE

Funny features
There are lots of different designs for you to try with the geometry shapes. Stick to the shapes only – don't be tempted to cheat! Remember to blow the excess chalk off your picture before you hang it up.

Use the geometry set shapes to exaggerate some of the features on your face, such as the eyes and the chin.

This rabbit's enormous ears were created with a triangle.

Use the outside and inside edges of a protractor for the rabbit's paws.

Use straight lines and sharp edges to give your monster a frightening face.

Make small teeth using the end of a large triangle.

Bewildered bunny
Add to the weirdness of your geometric picture with a wacky choice of colour to finish it off. Have you ever seen a blue and green rabbit with purple paws?

Metric monster
How about using the shapes to create your very own monster? You can make him as evil or as friendly as you like.

 Waste not, want not
Keep the excess chalk dust so that you can dab it around the edge of your picture.

ART ATTACK

TOP T-SHIRTS

Do you have any old, white T-shirts lying around in your drawers? Why not jazz them up with some brilliant do-it-yourself designs?

From plain to patterned

Materials
- White T-shirt and cardboard
- Pencil
- Black marker pen
- Gold and silver marker pens

1 Place a piece of cardboard inside a plain white T-shirt. This stretches the fabric, making it easier to draw on.

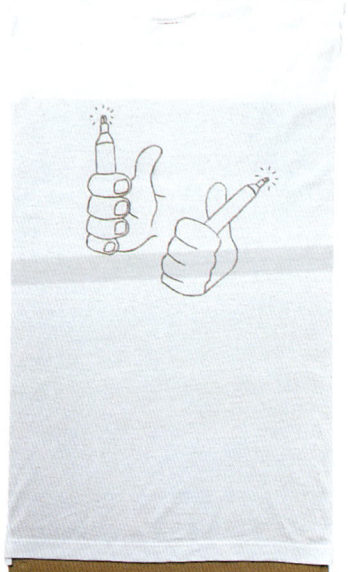

2 Sketch a rough design on the T-shirt in pencil, so you can change part of the design if you want to.

You can draw any design you like on your T-shirt.

3 Once you are happy with your pencil design, trace over it with a permanent marker pen. The cardboard inside the T-shirt will stop the ink from soaking through and staining the back of the T-shirt.

Be careful not to colour over the lines.

4 Your T-shirt is now ready to be coloured in. There are lots of different materials that you can use, such as fabric paint, acrylic paint, or even nail varnish. For this design, we've used gold and silver marker pens.

TOP T-SHIRTS

Marker pen madness
Marker pens get a thumbs up for a quick and easy way to brighten up a T-shirt!

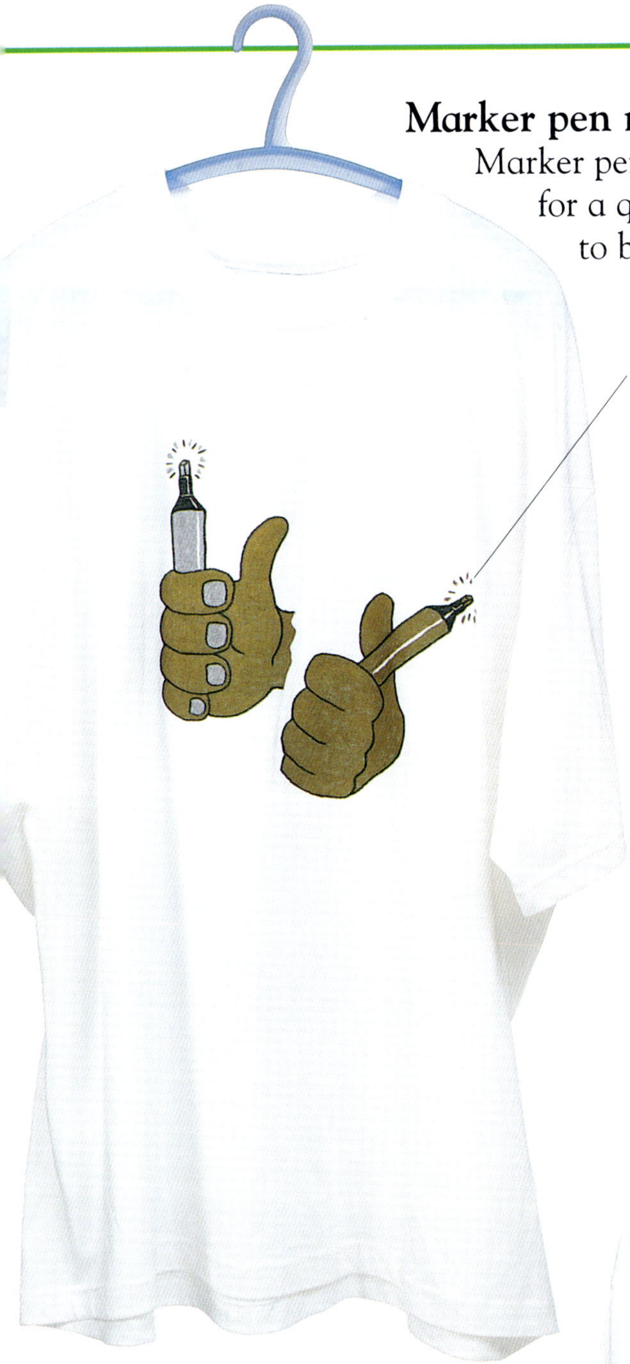

Make sure you use light, flicked strokes to avoid smearing.

Fabric paints are very brightly coloured and easy to use.

Busy bee
Fabric paints come in brilliant colours and will not fade too quickly. You could even touch up the design with some leftover nail varnish, which is waterproof.

Make sure your designs are big and bold so that they can be seen clearly when you wear the T-shirt.

Paint a special T-shirt for a friend's birthday with a personal design on it.

When the paint is dry, try designing an alien picture on the back too.

Washing care
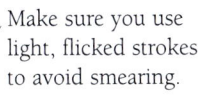
Always wash your T-shirt in a gentle wash so that the colours stay bright. Materials such as poster paints and felt-tip pens are likely to fade.

Lost in space
This design is perfect for a young space enthusiast! If you paint it with acrylic paints, remember to iron the T-shirt inside out when you have finished, to fix the colour.

27

ART ATTACK

NEAR AND FAR

Have you ever noticed how things look fainter the further away they get? It's a good tip to remember when you're creating pictures.

From card to mountain scene

Materials

Black card, tracing paper, and backing card

Scissors

1 Cut some rugged mountain shapes out of a sheet of black card. The mountain peaks should be near the top of the page. This will make them look larger in the finished picture. Place the card on a light background.

2 Take a piece of tracing paper and cut it to the same size as the card. Lay it on top of your mountain scene, making sure the black sheet is completely covered. You will notice that the mountain shapes have now faded.

Layer tip
Start by cutting the background scene at the top of the first card, and as you build up your layers cut further down the card each time. This will ensure that the first layers will seem further away in the distance.

3 Cut some tree shapes out of black card. Put the card on top of the tracing paper. The mountains will now seem further away and the trees closer. The layers will give your picture a feeling of depth.

4 Place another sheet of tracing paper on top of the tree shapes. Cut out the shape of a house on a hill. When you put the new card on top you will have three layers of depth and the mountains will seem even further away.

NEAR AND FAR

Distant landscape
Place another piece of tracing paper on top. Draw a gate and a wall on a piece of card, cut it out, and place it on your picture as the top layer. The mountain range is far away in the distance, and you have created perspective. Look over the gate and see for miles and miles!

To give your picture more depth, why not add even more layers of scenery?

Remember to let each stage dry before you begin a new layer.

Remote wilderness
Another brilliant way to create perspective is to paint a watered-down layered picture. For the first layer, mix together a lot of water and not much paint to create the idea of distance. When this layer is dry, paint the next stage using less water for a darker effect. Let the picture dry again, then paint the foreground even darker. Finally use the undiluted paint to draw in finer details. When it is dry, stand back and look into the distance!

The further away the moutains are, the paler they appear.

Draw the nearer balloon lower than the distant one.

Paint the ground nearest to you a darker colour.

Desert highway
The further away objects are, the smaller they appear. Paint a road using this tip. It will be very wide in the foreground and will get thinner as it travels into the distance. Add telegraph poles and a fence, which will also get smaller and closer together. Draw two balloons of different sizes, the bigger balloon will seem nearer. When you have finished, gaze down the never-ending highway!

ART ATTACK

POP-UP CARD

All your friends will love this pop-up novelty card! It's easy to make and much more fun to receive than an ordinary card.

From paper to pop-up card

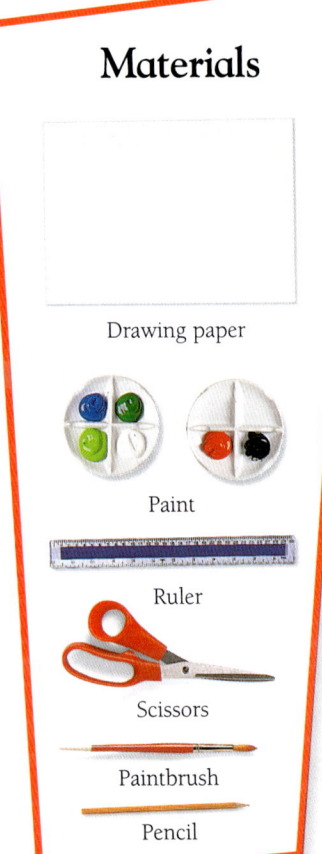

Materials

Drawing paper

Paint

Ruler

Scissors

Paintbrush

Pencil

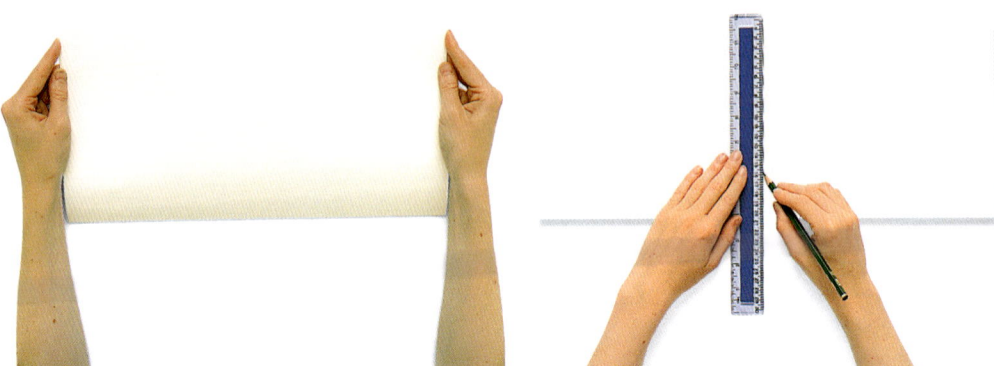

1 Take a sheet of drawing paper and fold it in half one way, matching up the edges of the paper. Then fold it in half again, matching the left and right sides together so that it looks like a greetings card.

2 With a pencil, draw a line down the fold on the inside of the card. You will use this line later to remind you which part is the inside of your card. Remember to rub it out before you paint the card!

Use a ruler to measure the line that you will cut.

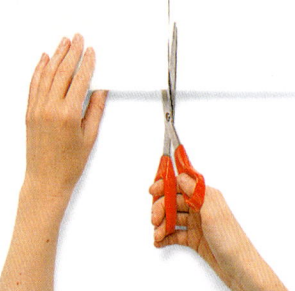

3 Make sure the pencil line is still on the inside of the fold. Measure a quarter of the way along the folded edge of the paper and mark it. Cut a straight line upwards from this mark, half way to the top.

4 Fold back the paper into triangle flaps, made by the cut. Crease them well along the edges. Unfold the flaps, turn the card over, and press in the same crease on the reverse side.

POP-UP CARD

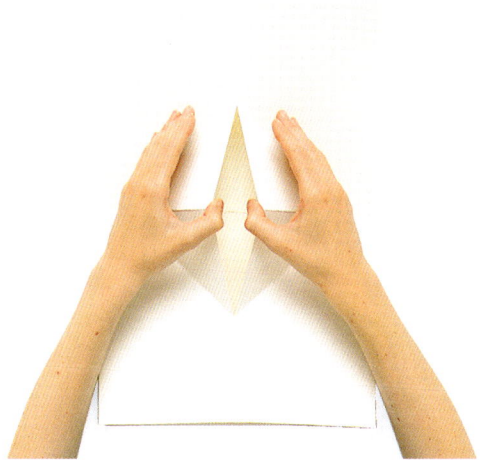

As the card starts to close, press down really hard on top of it, trapping the flaps open.

Draw the mouth first, then design the body around it.

5 Open out the sheet of paper. Fold the paper in half along your pencil line crease, making sure the line is on the inside of the card. Put your thumbs inside the slot and pull out the edges of the flaps. Close the card with the flaps open.

6 Open out the card and turn it so that the slot is horizontal, it should close like a mouth. Then draw a simple design on the card, such as a frog.

Wide-mouth frog
Decide on a background for your picture and then paint it in bright, bold colours. Remember to paint the inside of the mouth, too! You can send your card for a friend's birthday, or even just to say "hello"!

Friendly fish
Lots of different designs will look great as pop-ups, like this friendly fish.

A ghostly tale
Try making this spooky pop-up ghost for Halloween. Use lots of dark colours for a scary, haunted feel.

Make the mouth bigger or smaller by changing the length of the line you cut.

31

ART ATTACK

PEN PAL

Create your very own pen pal with some paint, modelling clay, and imagination! It looks fantastic, and it holds your favourite pens too!

From clay to pen pal

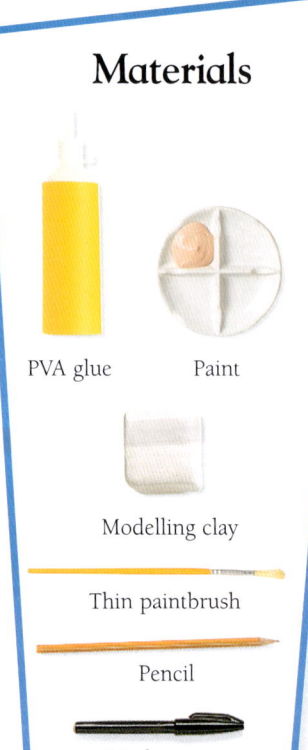

Materials

- PVA glue
- Paint
- Modelling clay
- Thin paintbrush
- Pencil
- Marker pen

Clay tip
Try and find modelling clay that will harden by simply leaving it to dry overnight. You can find it in most toy or hardware shops.

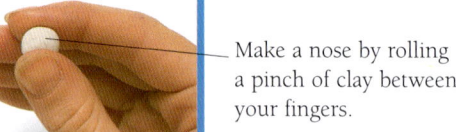

Make a nose by rolling a pinch of clay between your fingers.

1 Roll a piece of modelling clay in the palm of your hand. Make a small, shallow hole in the clay using a pen or a pencil.

2 Push the nose ball into the hole firmly to make sure it stays in place. Use a pencil to make two more holes above the nose for the eyes.

The clay will harden overnight, so make sure you have made all your holes before!

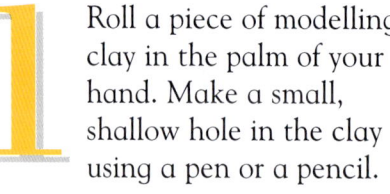

Paint carefully inside the holes so that no clay shows.

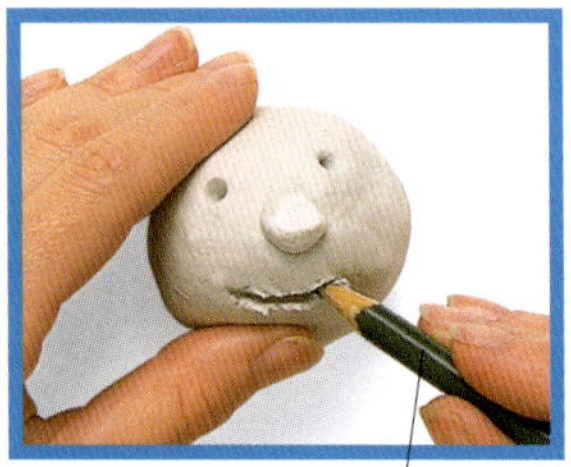

Make the mouth by scratching a line under the nose with a pencil.

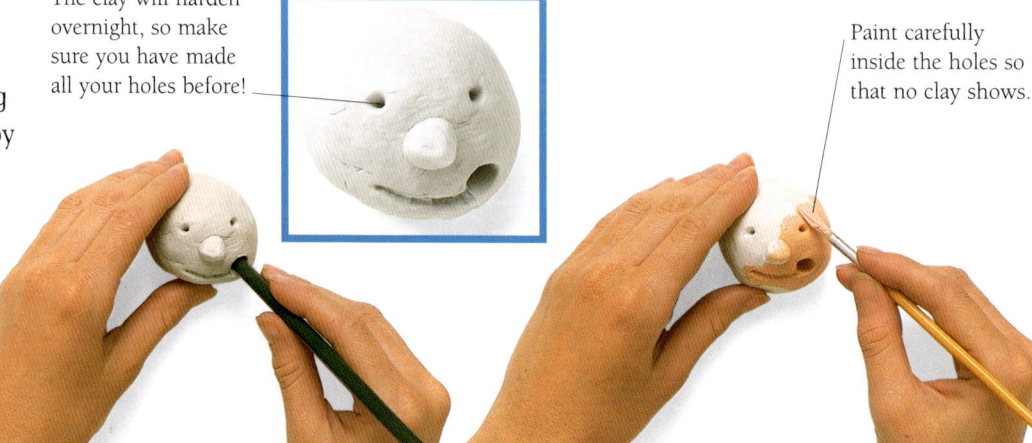

3 Mark a mouth with a pencil, then make the pen hole by pushing the pencil in at the side, about 3 cm deep. Twist it a little to open the hole.

4 Leave the pen pal to dry overnight. When it is hard, paint your model with poster paint. Make sure you cover it in paint and leave it to dry.

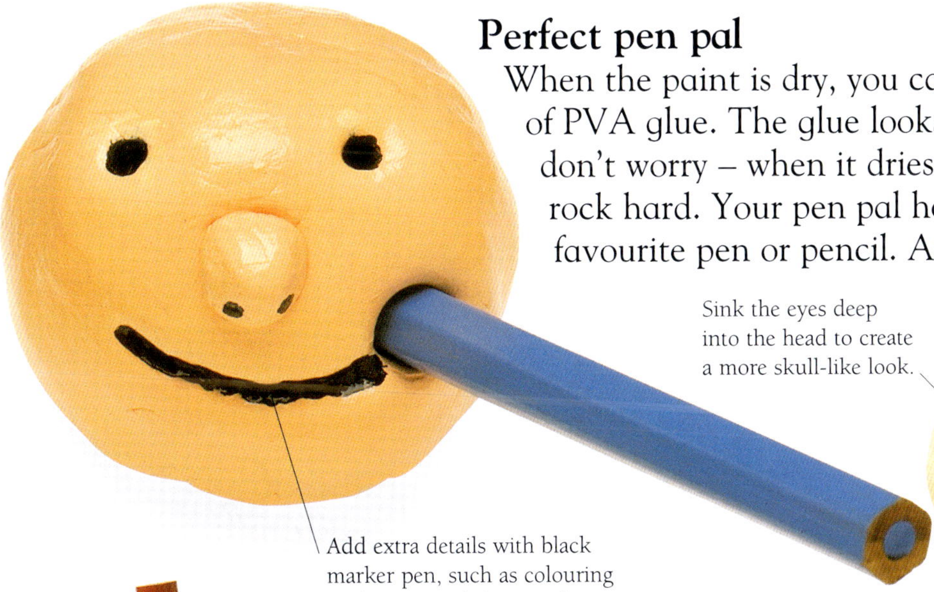

PEN PAL

Perfect pen pal
When the paint is dry, you can cover your pen pal with a coat of PVA glue. The glue looks white and creamy at first, but don't worry – when it dries it becomes smooth, shiny, and rock hard. Your pen pal holder is then ready to hold your favourite pen or pencil. After all, what are pen pals for?

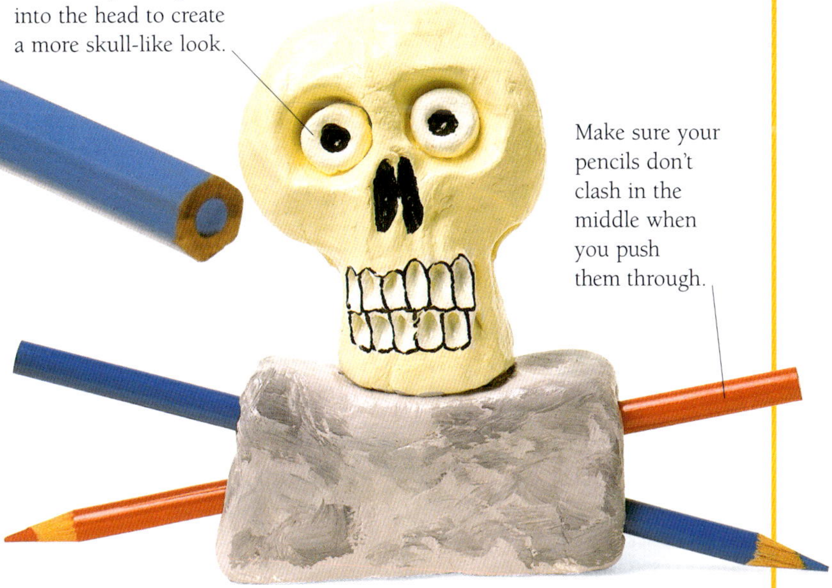

Sink the eyes deep into the head to create a more skull-like look.

Make sure your pencils don't clash in the middle when you push them through.

Add extra details with black marker pen, such as colouring in the eyes and the mouth.

Pink pig holder
The great thing about pen pals is that you can create as many different designs as you want, such as this pig. Try out your own ideas!

Make the ears by pinching some clay into triangles and curling them forwards.

Skull and crosspens!
To create this monster pen pal, shape the clay into a spooky skull and base. Your pencils will look just like crossbones!

Make sure the holes are deep enough so that the pencils don't topple out!

To make the pig's tail, roll a piece of clay into a sausage and twist it into shape.

Handy hedgehog
This hedgehog pen pal will carry a whole range of pens or pencils. The more holes you make, the more pencil prickles you will have! Try using lots of coloured pencils to make the pen holder really stand out.

Pen pal presents
Why not give your pen pals away? You can make lots and lots of pen pal holders from one block of modelling clay. They make perfect presents for your family and friends!

33

ART ATTACK

MAGIC MASK

What's a party for unless you can dress up? Here are some wonderful ways to impress your friends and get noticed wherever you go!

From balloon to mask

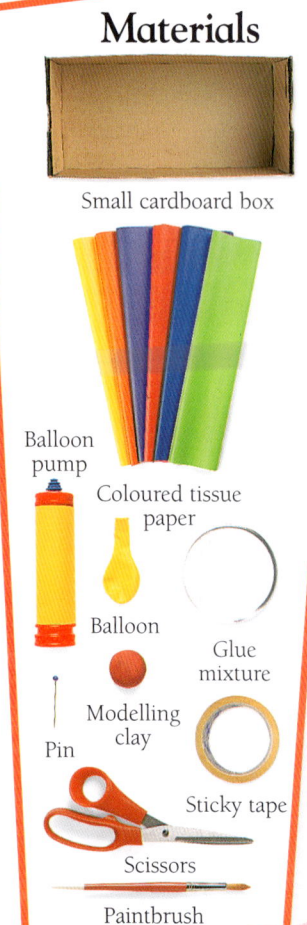

Materials
- Small cardboard box
- Coloured tissue paper
- Balloon pump
- Balloon
- Glue mixture
- Modelling clay
- Pin
- Sticky tape
- Scissors
- Paintbrush

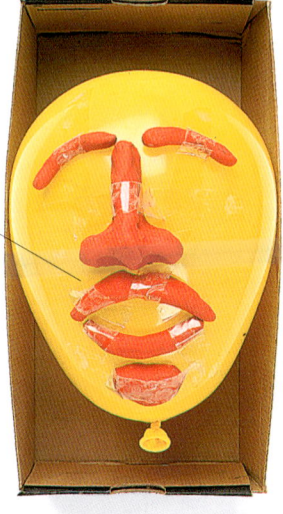

Make sure the balloon is roughly the same size as your own head.

1 Blow up a balloon and place it in a shoebox to keep it stable. The balloon will form the basic shape of your mask.

2 Use modelling clay to make the eyebrows, nose, mouth, and chin. Attach these shapes to the balloon with sticky tape.

Tissue tip
Make sure the tissue paper strips are long enough to create a really interesting border for your mask.

3 Cut long strips of differently coloured tissue paper and stick them over the whole face area using the glue mixture.

4 Build up the balloon with lots of layers of tissue paper. Leave to dry overnight and the tissue paper will turn hard and shiny.

MAGIC MASK

Fabulous faces
Remove the balloon and modelling clay from your mask. Now you have your very own multi-coloured tissue-paper mask to display on your wall!

The eyebrows and other features are raised.

Pop the balloon with a pin, but be careful, it may pop with a loud bang!

Glitter mask
You can decorate your masks in lots of ways. Try sprinkling on glitter and using brightly coloured sequins for a sparkly effect.

Try using layers of colours down the mask to create a stripy look.

Use different coloured glitter for the eyes and mouth.

Pierce the mask with a pencil before you cut out the eyes and mouth.

Stripy mask
Why not cut out holes in the eyes and the mouth so you can wear the mask? Your friends won't recognize you with it on!

35

ART ATTACK

FLOWER POWER

Who needs expensive garden centres when you can follow this terrific Art Attack and make some great 3-D flowers!

From paper to flower

Materials
- Coloured card
- Glue stick
- Sticky tape
- Scissors
- Marker pen

Cut about six more leaf shapes in a bright colour.

Make sure you hold the scissors very carefully when you score lines.

1 Take some green card and draw some flattened S-shape squiggles on it with a pen. Draw a leaf shape around each of the squiggles.

2 Wrap sticky tape around the end of your scissor blades. Carefully, but firmly, score the scissors along the centre line, but don't cut through the card.

The paper will crease easily along the scored line creating a 3-D effect.

Cut a slit from the edge of the circle to the centre, glue along the edge of one of the flaps, and stick it down into a cone shape.

3 Cut the leaves out and crease them along the scored line. Draw a stalk shape and score a line down the middle of it. Cut it out, and crease along the centre line.

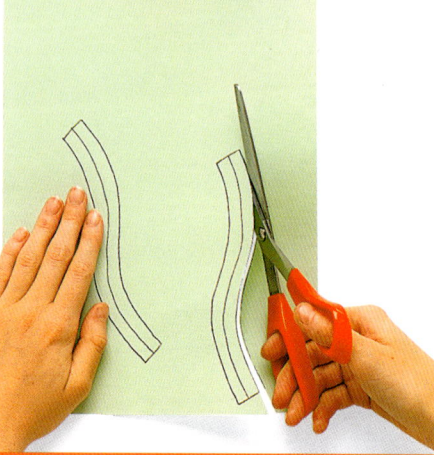

4 Make the centre of your flower from a circle of different coloured paper. Lay your stalk down on some backing card and place the cone-shaped centre on the top of the stalk.

36

FLOWER POWER

Folded paper plant

Experiment using different colours and arrange the petals into different shapes to create unusual flowers. Try making several different kinds and then put them together to create a whole bunch!

The folds give the leaves a really good 3-D effect.

Draw extra details, such as birds, on your picture with a pen.

Sunny scene

Why not try making other folded paper designs, such as this sunny beach scene? Make important aspects of the picture, such as the sun and the sand dunes, 3-D so that they really stand out from the rest of the picture.

Choose a contrasting colour for your background card.

You can make the petals any shape you like.

Take care not to crush each piece as you stick it down.

5 Make some different coloured petals in the same way as the leaves. Making sure you have creased the shapes well, arrange the leaves, petals, stalk, and centre on to the backing card before you stick them down.

6 When you're happy with the arrangement of the pieces, gently stick the shapes on to the backing card. Glue only the sides of each piece. Make sure you keep the 3-D shape by not flattening them.

37

ART ATTACK

GLITTER FUN

For this fantastic Art Attack, you paint a picture, not with paint, but with glue. Then you add some glitter for that extra sparkle!

Materials

Coloured paper
Glitter
PVA glue
Rubber
Cotton bud
Pencil

From glue to glitter

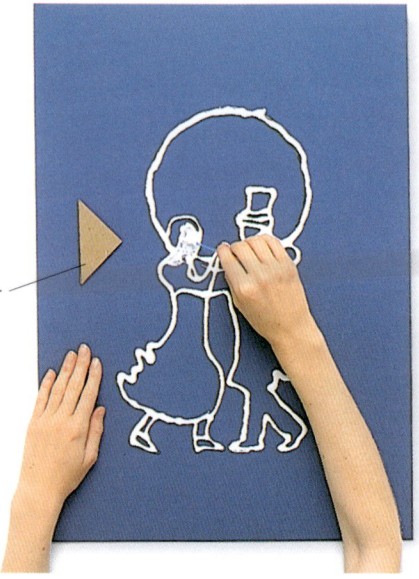

Keep the cardboard handy so you can use it on the larger areas.

1 Draw a picture on a piece of paper or card in pencil. Spread some glue over the areas you want to cover with glitter, making sure you don't go over the lines.

2 Use a piece of cardboard to spread the glue over the bigger areas. Try using a cotton bud for the smaller, more fiddly areas.

Create your own pink glitter by mixing gold, silver, and red glitter.

You can make the pink glitter darker by adding more blue glitter.

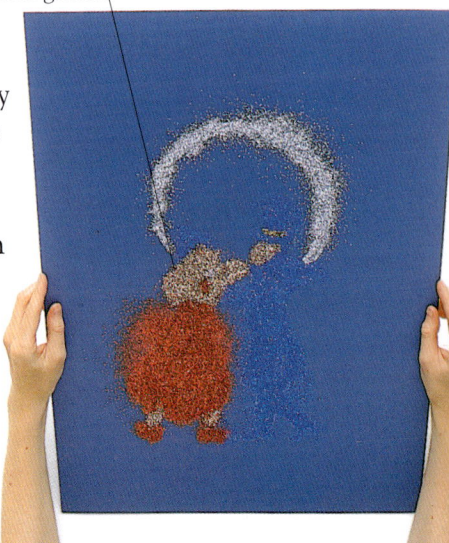

3 Decide which colours you want to use. While the glue is still wet, sprinkle the coloured glitter over the glued areas. Don't worry about being too neat, just make sure you cover all the glue with glitter.

4 Allow the picture to dry and the glue should soak up all the glitter. Now for the fun part! Simply tip the picture up and shake it until all the excess glitter has come off. Make sure you've covered the area with newspaper first!

GLITTER FUN

Ballroom beauties
Against the dark colour of the background card, the two ballroom dancers look stunning as they sparkle and twirl around the floor.

Turn the lights down low, just like in a real ballroom, and see your picture glow.

For maximum effect use contrasting colours, such as this dark blue and vivid red.

Pick out the detail on the guitar with silver or gold glitter.

All that jazz
What about making a funky musical picture? Draw your favourite instruments and then dot musical notes around the picture for some swinging sparkle!

Exotic parrot
Try making several glitter pictures to brighten up your bedroom walls, such as this exotic parrot perched among the lush green leaves of its tropical rainforest home.

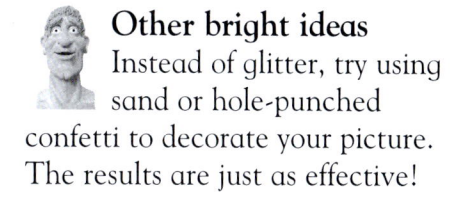

Other bright ideas
Instead of glitter, try using sand or hole-punched confetti to decorate your picture. The results are just as effective!

39

ART ATTACK

LIGHT AND DARK

Have you ever tried drawing a dark room? It's simple! All you have to do is let in a tiny bit of light and watch what happens!

From dark to light

Materials

Black paper

White chalk

1 Taking some white chalk and a piece of black paper, begin by letting some light into the bedroom by opening a door. Draw three sides of an open door on the left side of the paper.

2 Now you need to let some light into the room. Use your finger to smudge the chalk away from the door. Try to make your smudges straight as light falls in straight lines.

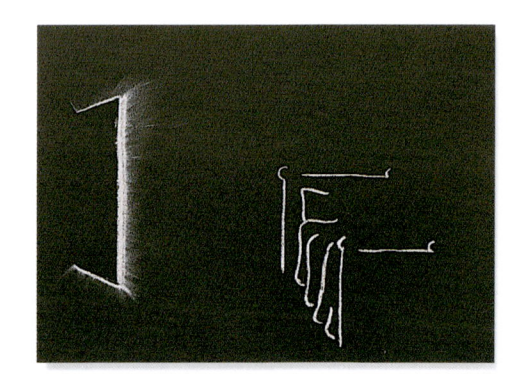

Shadow tip
Always remember which direction the light is coming from when you draw your pictures. Why not practise by shining a lamp on an object and finding out where the shadows fall?

3 Now there is light in the bedroom, you can see how it falls on the furniture. You can see only one side of the objects so draw the bed by outlining the side nearest the door.

4 Where you have drawn curved shapes, such as the sheets, soften the line by smudging the chalk. Always remember to brush the chalk away from the door, or light source.

40

LIGHT AND DARK

Shining light

Draw in some extra furniture to finish off your bedroom and see how effective it can be when you use light and dark. Why not draw your own room? You could even test the light by opening the door in your bedroom a little and looking to see where the light falls.

Make sure you remember to only draw the sides that are nearest the light.

Shadowy street scene

Another way to show light and dark is to add shadows to a picture. The way to find out where shadows fall is to look for the places that light can't get to. On a dark sheet of paper, use chalk to draw a night scene with a lamppost. Follow the light from the lamp and put shadows in the places that don't get any light – down the left side of the man and half way up the wall.

Draw in the light by smudging white chalk on the lamppost.

Make sure you draw the trees smaller the further away they get.

Moonlight silhouettes

Use white chalk to draw a moon and some fluffy cloud edges. Using black chalk, draw in some lines as tree shapes. Shade the edges of the trees that face away from the light. With white chalk, highlight the sides that catch the light. Draw shadows on the ground where the light can't get to. The moon gives an eerie light to the wood.

41

ART ATTACK

CREASED ART

Here's a great way of literally making your artwork jump straight off the page – by crunching up paper!

Materials

Wrapping paper, backing card, and coloured paper

Newspaper

Kitchen foil

Glue stick   Glue mixture

Scissors

Paintbrush

Marker pen

From paper to art

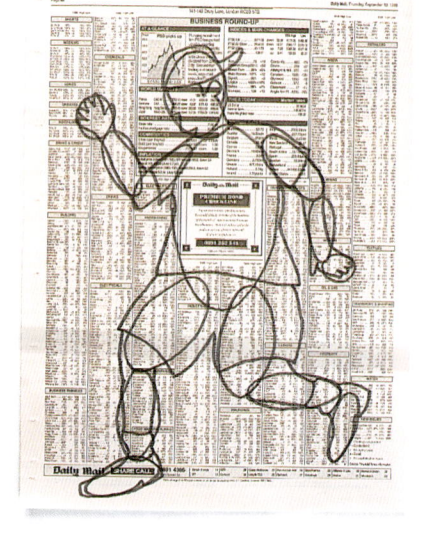

1 Take a page of newspaper and draw a person on it. It's a good idea to draw the person in sausage shapes first, to get the right positions.

2 Once you're happy with the body, draw clothes on your person, such as a baseball cap, T-shirt, some shorts, socks, and nice big trainers.

Don't be afraid to crunch up the paper tightly to make them really creased!

3 Cut out all the pieces separately. Use them as templates and draw around them on different coloured paper, such as kitchen foil or wrapping paper. Cut the coloured shapes out.

4 Brush glue mixture onto all the pieces of paper and leave them to dry. When they are dry, they should be hard and shiny. Crunch up each one in your hands to put lots of creases in them.

CREASED ART

5 When you have crunched up each piece, practise laying them on to some backing card in their right positions. Piece them all back together like a jigsaw.

6 Stick the pieces down by lightly placing a couple of dabs of glue at the edge of each one. Take care not to flatten them as you do this, or you will spoil the 3-D effect.

In the groove
Try adding other decorations in the background, such as these musical notes in black marker pen, or even some kitchen foil shine for a really funky look.

Soccer star
You can use this technique to create pictures of anything – from a famous sports person, to a pop star, or even your favourite toy!

The creased art effect makes this footballer look as if he's really running after the ball.

The musical notes add to the effect of the figure dancing.

Superman's cape billows in the wind as he dashes through the sky on another adventure.

Brightly coloured backing board really sets off the main picture.

Super hero!
Creasing the paper makes your artwork literally jump off the page! Superman in 3-D!

43

ART ATTACK

3-D SCENE

Create an unusual effect by making these amazing see-through pictures. Layer them up and watch how they become 3-D!

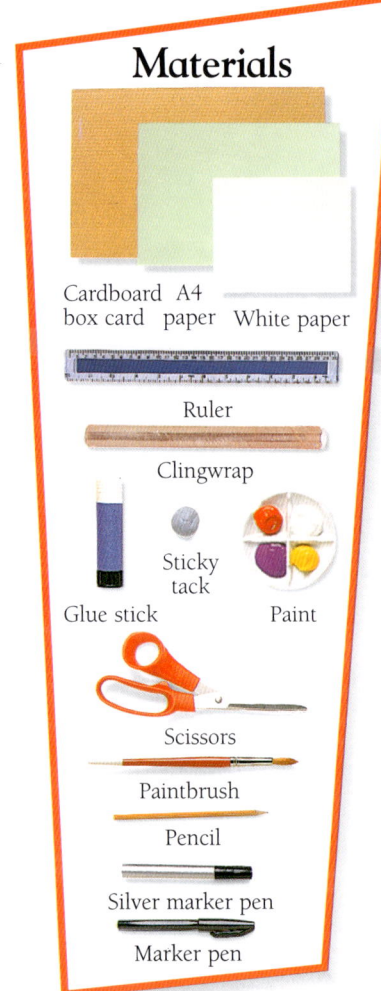

From cardboard to 3-D picture

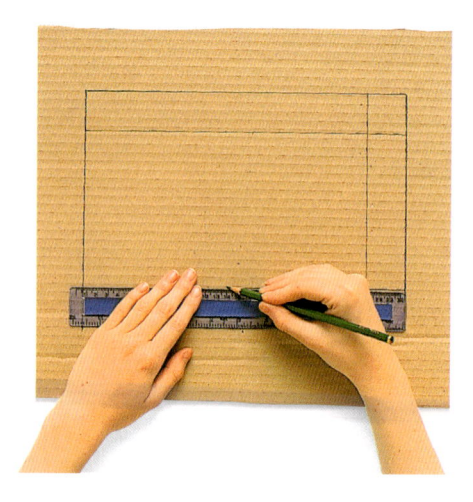

Materials
- Cardboard box
- A4 card paper
- White paper
- Ruler
- Clingwrap
- Glue stick
- Sticky tack
- Paint
- Scissors
- Paintbrush
- Pencil
- Silver marker pen
- Marker pen

1 Start by making the first see-through picture. Place a piece of A4 paper in the centre of a big piece of cardboard. Carefully draw around the paper with a pencil.

2 Place a ruler against one of the inside edges of the rectangle and draw along it. Do the same along all the edges of the rectangle, so that you end up with a frame shape.

Top heavy
It's a good idea to place some heavy books on top of the cardboard frames as they dry, to really press them together.

5 Apply glue to the other cardboard frame and press the two frames together so that the clingwrap is sandwiched in between. When the glue is dry, trim off the excess clingwrap.

6 While you are waiting for your frame to dry, practise your design on a piece of paper so that you can then correct any mistakes that you may make. For the best effect, keep your picture very simple.

3-D SCENE

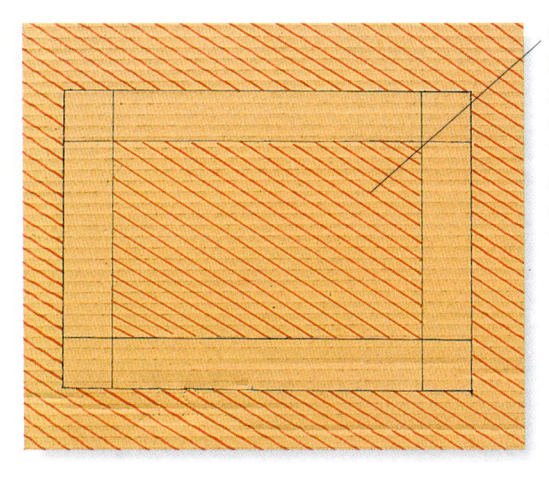

Cut out the red, hatched area by making a hole in the cardboard with a pencil, and then pushing scissors through the hole.

Smooth down the edges with your fingertips.

Take your time with this stage – it is important to roll the clingwrap smoothly.

3 Your frame should be A4 in size and one ruler width thick. Cut it out and then repeat the whole procedure, so that you end up with two frames which are exactly the same size.

4 Apply some glue mixture over the surface of one frame. Stick some clingwrap down on one end and then roll it out to cover the whole frame. Press the clingwrap on to the glue and gently stretch it to smooth out all the wrinkles. The clingwrap should be taut.

Add wispy lines to the frame for a wood-grain effect and paint silver dots to look like screws.

7 Place your picture under the clingwrap frame and trace the design using a permanent marker pen. Just draw the basic shape at this stage, because you can add more detail when you paint it later.

8 Your picture is now ready to be painted. Use either acrylic paint, or poster paint with some washing-up liquid mixed in it to make it stick to the clingwrap. Add little bits of detail to make your picture look realistic.

45

ART ATTACK

IN THE FRAME

To make your see-through picture 3-D, simply make three pictures! Lay the frames on top of each other and stand back to admire the effect!

Paint a complete picture on the bottom frame to create a background.

To create a night-time feeling, paint the bottom layer dark with bright yellow lights and a moon.

Clingwrap is very thin, so be careful not to puncture a hole in it as you paint on your pictures.

Outline the details of your picture in black marker pen to help them stand out.

The middle layer of your picture should be only half painted on so that you can see the background behind it.

Night watch
When you have finished painting each picture, place them on top of each other and stand back to admire your amazing 3-D effect! If you stick them together with sticky tack you could even change the pictures around to create a totally different look each time.

Use bright yellow paint to give the effect of a lit streetlamp.

Paint only a few pictures on the top layer so that they will look as if they are in the foreground.

IN THE FRAME

You could design any scene you want. Why not try painting a scene near your home?

A bright picture in the foreground of a night-time scene will really stand out.

Counting sheep

The more cardboard boxes you have, the more frames you can paint. Why not try putting four or five paintings together to create a really big, see-through picture for your wall?

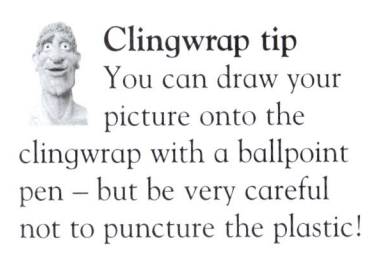

Clingwrap tip
You can draw your picture onto the clingwrap with a ballpoint pen – but be very careful not to puncture the plastic!

47

ART ATTACK

IN A FLAP

Here's a bit of fun! Does this look like an ordinary picture? Well, just open it up... and surprise – one half of the picture has changed!

From paper to greeting card

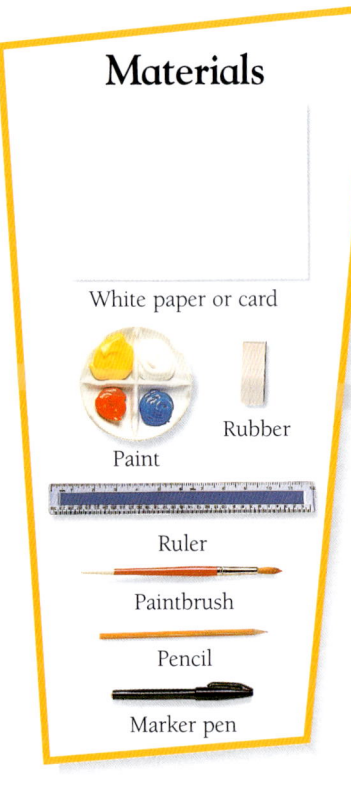

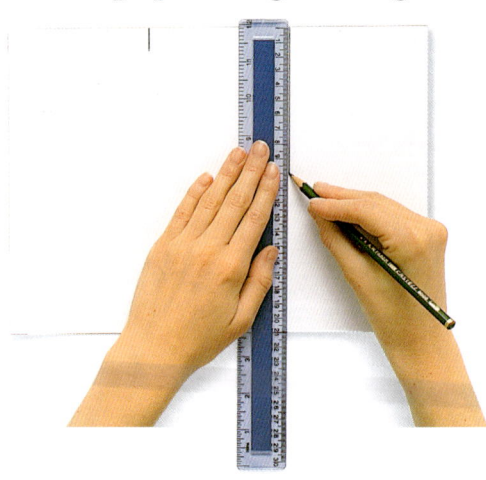

Materials
White paper or card
Paint
Rubber
Ruler
Paintbrush
Pencil
Marker pen

1 Take a piece of paper or thin card and divide it up roughly into three. Draw a line down the right hand divide and fold the paper along this line.

2 With the flap closed draw a picture on the paper and across the flap. Draw half of a person's face on the paper and the other half on the flap.

Draw the bits you don't want to change first, so you can concentrate on the surprise last.

Simple scene Keep your picture simple and cartoon-like for the most effective surprise effect.

3 Open out the flap and complete the picture there, too. This time, however, make a huge change to the picture.

4 When you are happy with the surprise you have created inside the flap, colour in your picture, including both sides of the flap, using lots of bright paints.

48

IN A FLAP

What a shock!
A picture you can open with a surprise inside! And wouldn't you look surprised if, while out for a quiet day's fishing, you came face-to-face with a huge shark!

By painting one half of the face on the paper and the other half on the flap, you can change the person's expression when the flap is opened out.

Watch out!
A pleasant day in the country, spent smelling the flowers, but look out – there's a ferocious bull behind you!

Why not send your cards to mark a special occasion?

ART ATTACK

ON THE EDGE

Here's a really good way of creating an original decorative border for almost anything! Simply cut out bright pictures from old magazines or comics.

From magazine to frame

Materials
- Coloured card and mirror tile★
- Sticky tack
- Comic or old magazine
- PVA glue
- Glue stick
- Scissors
- Thin paintbrush
- Marker pen

1 Draw around a mirror tile on a piece of card. Choose some pictures from an old magazine or comic for your border and cut them out.

2 Remove the mirror tile and stick the pictures on the line with a glue stick. Paint over the pictures with PVA glue to make them shiny.

Cut out the hatched areas marked in red.

Press the border down firmly to ensure that it sticks to the mirror.

Border tip
When you position your magazine cut-outs on the card, cover the line completely with pictures so that the edges of your mirror will not show when the border is in place.

3 When the glue is dry, cut out your border. Make sure you cut out the area inside and outside your border and be careful not to cut through the pictures.

4 Stick some sticky tack on the back of your border, and position it onto the mirror. Make sure you cover the edges of the mirror tile.

★ *Always be careful when handling mirror tiles or objects with sharp edges.*

ON THE EDGE

Mirror, mirror on the wall
What a fantastic way of jazzing up a dull, old mirror tile, simply by adding some bright pictures as a border! Stand back and admire yourself in your brilliant magazine-framed mirror!

Try theming your borders. You could use cartoon characters, animals, or even vegetables!

Tile tip
You can find mirror tiles in most DIY or hardware shops. Mirror card, however, can look just as effective as a shiny alternative.

Make a sign for your bedroom door. You could even put your name in the centre.

Overlap the pictures to make the border look really busy.

Top tape boxes
There are lots of other ways to use magazine cut-outs. Try cutting out pictures of your favourite pop stars to cover your tape boxes.

Collect pictures of pop stars and when you have enough, stick them on!

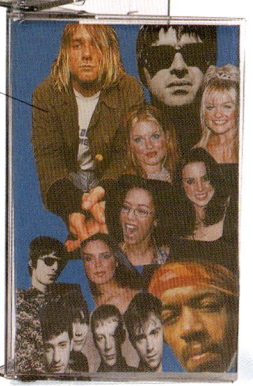

Why not cut out pictures of your favourite hobby?

Animal magic
There are lots of different themes you can experiment with, and lots of different magazines you can look through. You could frame a sign for your bedroom or even decorate your own greetings cards. Try your own different designs. The choices are endless!

51

ART ATTACK

GRIM GARGOYLE

Are you fed up with people bursting into your bedroom without knocking first? If so, then what you need is an angry doorknocker!

From cardboard to doorknocker

Materials
- Cardboard and newspaper
- Sticky tape
- Pebbles
- PVA glue mixture
- String
- Kitchen paper
- Paint
- Scissors
- Tissue paper
- Marker pen

The dots mark the areas where you will attach the knocker to the face.

Do not cover the pebble or the mouth shape with the kitchen paper.

1 Draw a gargoyle face with an angry mouth on a piece of cardboard and cut it out. Mark four dots on the upper lip, two above and two below.

2 To build up the facial features, scrunch up balls of kitchen paper in a glue mixture, and stick them to the face. Tape a small pebble to the lower lip.

3 When it is hard and dry, paint the face black. Let it dry. Dip a ball of tissue paper into a lighter paint and dab it on. Make holes through the four dots on the mouth – these are for attaching the knocker to the face.

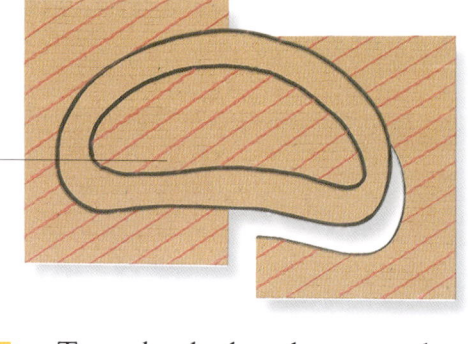

Cut out the hatched areas marked in red.

4 To make the knocker, copy the shape of the gargoyle's mouth onto a piece of cardboard. Cut the shape out. It should fit on the gargoyle's face perfectly.

GRIM GARGOYLE

Ghastly gargoyle doorknocker
Make sure the pebbles line up so that the knock is extra loud! Attach it to your door so that anyone who dares to enter is confronted by an angry knocker!

Make the face uglier with extra big features, such as the nose and the teeth.

Try using bronze or brown paint – it's a great way to make the gargoyles look really old.

Hide the string by painting it the same colour as the knocker.

Monster features
Gargoyles are traditionally very ugly creatures, so you can make the face as horrible as possible!

The more kitchen paper you use on the cardboard, the more 3-D it will be.

Scary skull
There are all sorts of different shapes you can experiment with. Why not try making a skull to scare away unwanted visitors!

Wrap tape tightly around the knocker.

Make sure the pebble lines up with the one on the face.

Tie the string in tight knots at the back of the gargoyle.

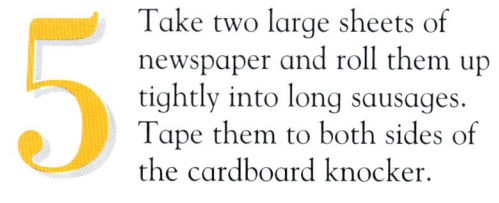

5 Take two large sheets of newspaper and roll them up tightly into long sausages. Tape them to both sides of the cardboard knocker.

6 Tape a pebble to the lower lip. Cover the knocker with kitchen paper, using glue mixture, leaving the pebble free. Paint the knocker.

7 Attach the knocker by threading some string through the holes on the upper lip. Tie the string firmly.

53

ART ATTACK

SWINGY SPIDER

Discover how to make paper literally spring into life with these mad spider mobiles, which wobble when you shake them!

From paper to mobile

Materials
- Coloured card and paper
- String
- Sticky tape
- Paint
- Rubber
- Scissors
- Pencil
- Paintbrush
- Marker pen

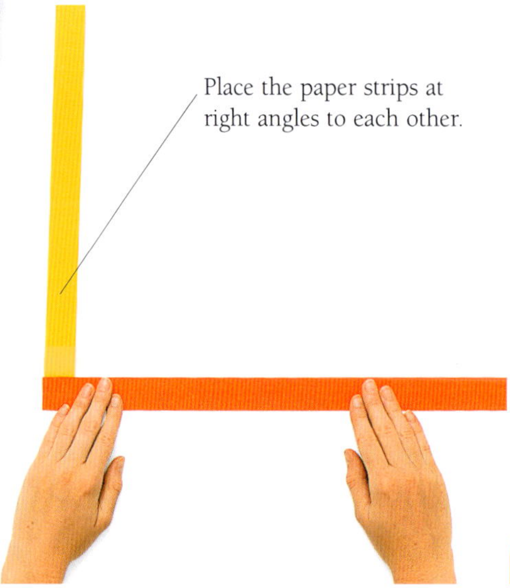

Place the paper strips at right angles to each other.

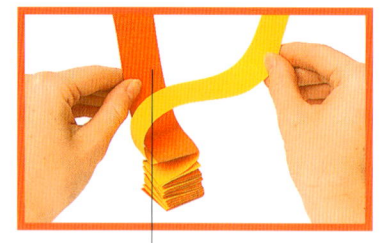

Always fold the bottom strip up and over the top strip.

1 Cut two long, thin strips of different coloured paper. Place one strip across the other to form an "L" shape and tape the two ends.

2 Fold the paper strips over each other until you get to the end of each strip. Trim the strips and fix the ends together. Repeat this four times.

Add features such as eyebrows to make your spider's face really expressive.

Paint one side first and then let it dry before you paint the other side.

3 Draw the shape of a spider's hairy body and its eight feet on some coloured card. You may want to do this stage in pencil first, so you can make changes or correct any mistakes. Then cut out the shapes.

4 Paint in your spider's eyes and add detail to its body. Make sure you fill in both the front and the back, so that when the mobile is hanging up, it can be seen from both sides.

SWINGY SPIDER

Mad mobile!
Punch a hole in the top of the spider, thread some string through, and hang it from the ceiling. Then watch the legs wobble when you shake it!

Striped terror
How about this for a scary spider? With those fearsome eyes and jagged, spiky edges, you can make a really ferocious mobile!

The longer you make the legs, the more effective your mobile will look.

If you make a few spiders, they look great as party decorations.

These black and yellow stripes add to the spider's fierce look!

Jolly green giant
The soft outline and drooping eyelids give this spider a much friendlier air.

Stick the feet together with tape before you attach them.

Check the positions of all the legs before you stick them to the body.

5 Stick two of the foot shapes to the bottom of each leg. If you want to make your legs longer, simply repeat steps one and two and stick the two lengths together.

6 Make sure you are happy with the designs on the front and back of your spider's body. Attach the legs by sticking them on to one side with sticky tape. Ensure that they are fixed securely.

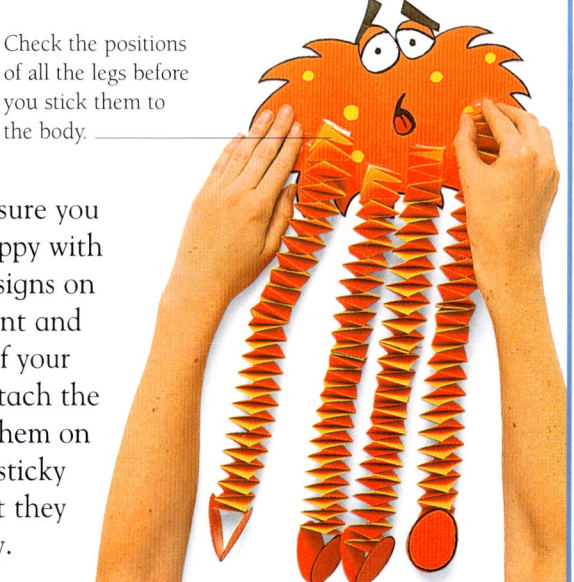

55

ART ATTACK

COLOUR WAVES

Here's a sort of 3-D wave that plays tricks on your eyes. To make it really effective, stick it on to a piece of contrasting backing card.

Materials

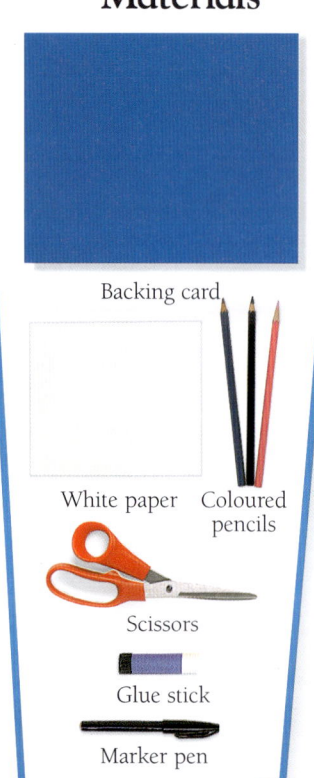

Backing card

White paper

Coloured pencils

Scissors

Glue stick

Marker pen

From paper to 3-D pattern

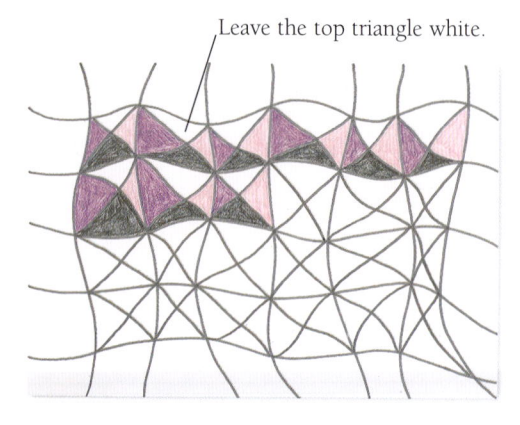

Leave the top triangle white.

1 Take a sheet of white paper and draw a criss-cross pattern of wavy lines. Place a wobbly cross inside each square.

2 Colour the squares using black in the bottom triangle, and two shades of the same colour for the left and right.

Only colour in the squares that do not border the edge of the paper.

Roll back the edges of the shorter sides of the wavy pattern, to create 3-D curls.

Colouring tip
It's very easy to make a mistake by colouring in the wrong triangle! Why not first put a small dot of the right colour in all the triangles so that you don't go wrong.

3 It is important to colour each square in exactly the same way to make the picture really effective. When you have finished, cut out the coloured pattern.

4 Stick your pattern on to a piece of contrasting backing. Complete the 3-D wave by pushing the edges of the sheet of paper inwards from both sides.

COLOUR WAVES

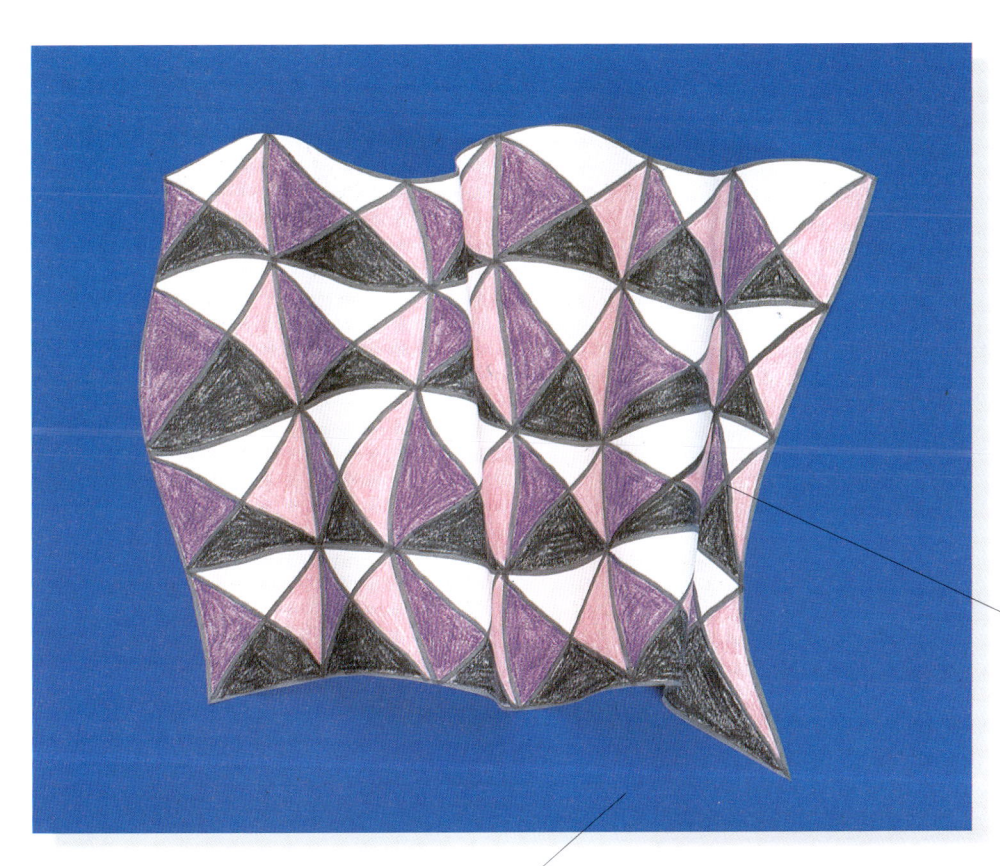

Waves of colour

The more you bend the paper into waves, the more effective your wavy pattern will look. Glue the underside of the paper between each wave so that the waves really stand up. Hang your picture on a wall and admire your very own 3-D wavy pattern!

You can also use paints to decorate your 3-D triangles.

Put your picture on the wall and impress your friends with your weird, wavy pattern.

It's important to have a bright colour as the backgound so that the waves really show up.

Folding frenzy

Try experimenting with the paper folds by making them as big or small as you like. Why not have a really big fold at the top and a small one at the bottom?

The more squares you draw, the more wavy your picture will be.

Wave variations

Make lots of your own wavy patterns, but remember to keep to the same colour theme on each one. For the most effective look use black, white, and two shades of the same colour. Have fun making waves!

57

ART ATTACK

VIDEO CITY

Do you ever have trouble finding your videos when they are all mixed up or in the wrong boxes? If so, what you need is a video city!

From boxes to city

Materials
- Cardboard and newspaper
- Video cassette box
- Paint
- Wide sticky tape
- PVA glue
- Scissors
- Thin paintbrush
- Gold and silver marker pens 
- Marker pen

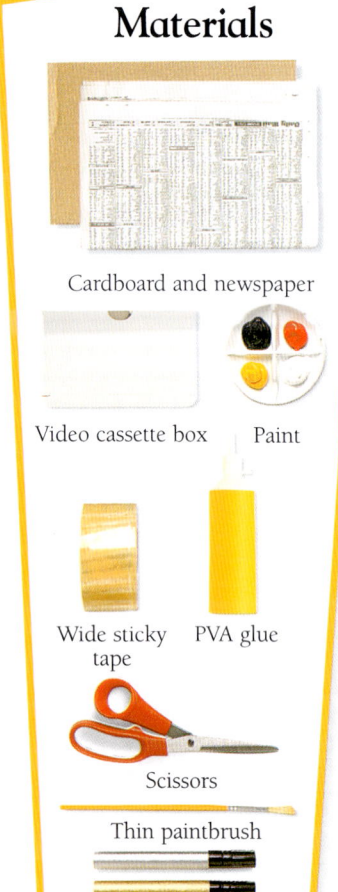

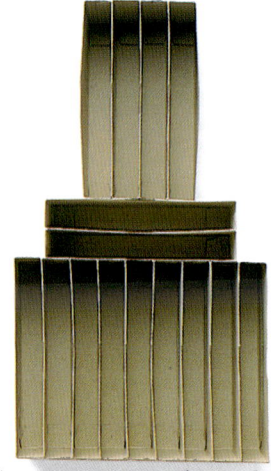

1 Arrange a number of empty video boxes in the shape of a skyscraper. Then glue the sides of the boxes together using PVA glue.

2 Place your skyscraper on top of a piece of thick cardboard and draw around it. Cut around the outline – this will be the front flap of your model.

The glue will turn hard and shiny as it dries.

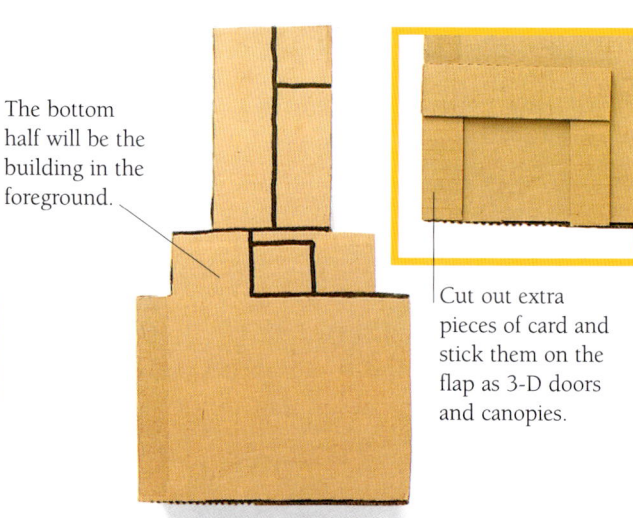

The bottom half will be the building in the foreground.

Cut out extra pieces of card and stick them on the flap as 3-D doors and canopies.

Video tip
When you cover the boxes with newspaper, make sure you leave the thumb grooves on the edge of the boxes free, so you can remove the videos easily.

5 Brush glue along the sides, back, and top of the video skyscraper and stick on strips of newspaper. Leave the front flap totally uncovered.

6 When your model is dry, draw lines on the uncovered front flap in black pen. These represent the different buildings on your video city.

VIDEO CITY

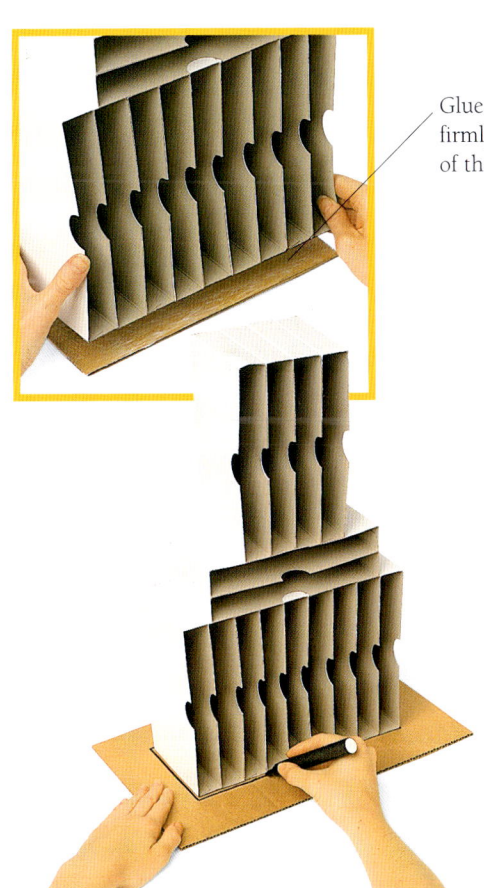

Glue the base shape firmly to the bottom of the video city.

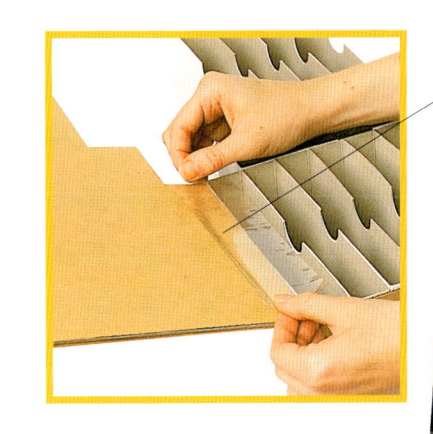

To make the flap stronger, open it up and tape it along the inside edge too.

Make sure you only tape this side, otherwise the door will not open.

Tape tip
When you are taping the front flap to the video city, it is a good idea to use really wide tape. Use lots of layers to hold it securely.

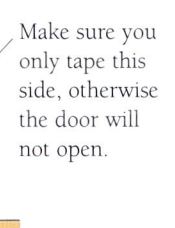

3 To ensure a firm base on your video city, stand the skyscraper on some cardboard and draw around the bottom of it using a marker pen. Cut out the shape and glue it to the base.

4 Once the glue has dried, lay your skyscraper on its back, and place the cardboard flap over the front of the video boxes. Attach it with tape along the lower half of the left side.

The lighter shades of grey give the impression of other buildings in the distance.

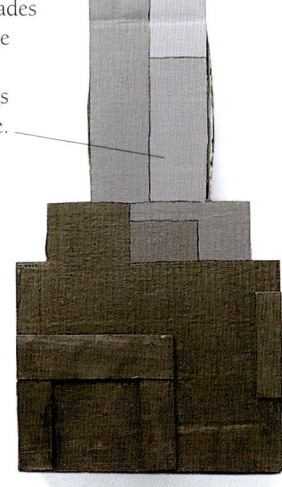

Paint the inside of the front flap black.

If you use poster paint, add a little PVA glue to it when you paint over the sticky tape, to make it hold.

7 On the front flap, paint the bottom section black and use lighter shades of grey towards the top. Paint the sides, back, and top of the model black.

8 Finish your city by painting in details, such as windows and signs. Colour them in oranges, yellows, or whites using acrylic or poster paints.

59

ART ATTACK

CITY LIGHTS

When the decoration is complete, your video city is ready to use. Fill the buildings up with your cassettes and display your dazzling skyscraper city.

Painting tip
Both acrylic and poster paints are easy to use and have a smooth finish. You can mix several colours to create lots of new shades.

Sparkling city
The decoration will take a long time, especially the small windows, but remember that the more carefully you work on them the more effective they will be. Take your time and go for the flashiest and busiest city you can!

Gold and silver pens are great to use for decoration. They help give a sparkling, night-time effect.

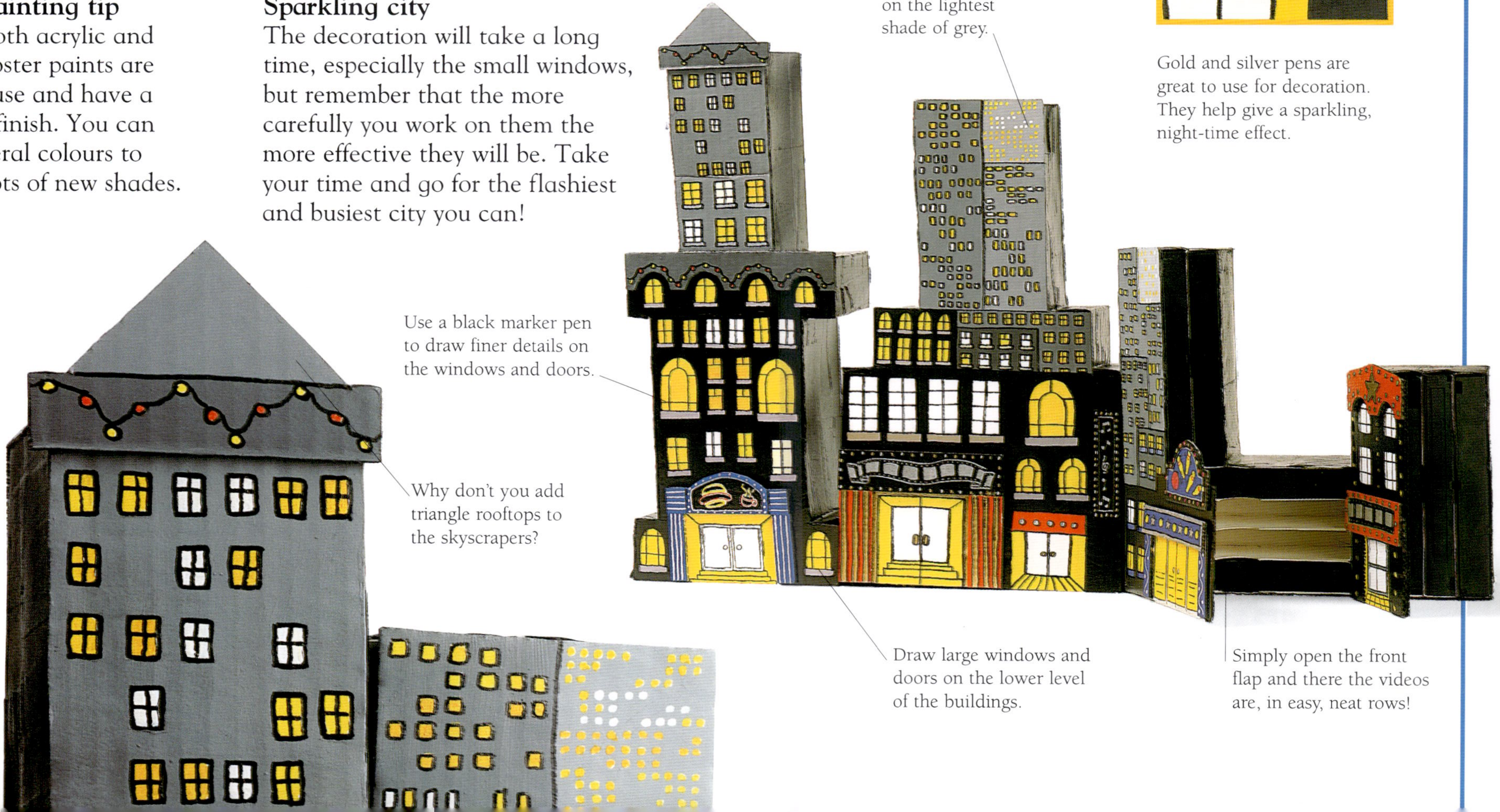

Simply open the front flap and there the videos are, in easy, neat rows!

Draw large windows and doors on the lower level of the buildings.

Paint very small windows on the lightest shade of grey.

Use a black marker pen to draw finer details on the windows and doors.

Why don't you add triangle rooftops to the skyscrapers?

60

CITY LIGHTS

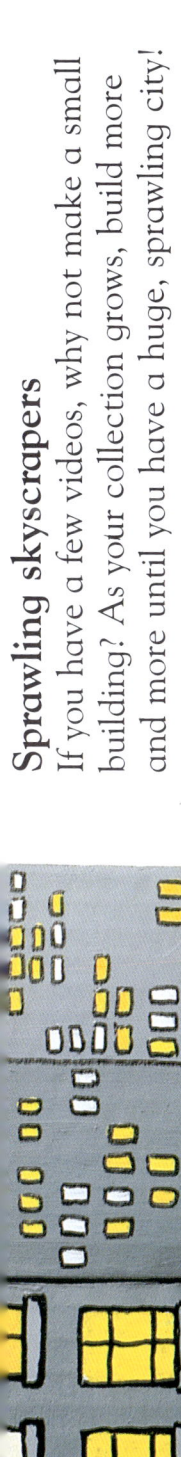

Sprawling skyscrapers

If you have a few videos, why not make a small building? As your collection grows, build more and more until you have a huge, sprawling city!

Make a sign or a triangle rooftop by cutting the shape out of cardboard and decorating it. Attach it to the front flap by gluing it to the inside.

Why not theme the shop fronts on your city structure? You could add a cinema, a bowling alley, or even a burger bar!

HANDY TIPS

There are lots of top tips and handy hints on this page that will help you when you are making the Art Attacks in this book.

Scoring on card
Tape together the ends of a pair of closed scissors. Press firmly to score a line, but do not tear the paper.

Making a hole in card
Place some modelling clay under the card. Press a sharp pencil through the card into the clay to make a neat hole.

Split pins
Push the pin through the hole, separate the two ends, and firmly press them flat.

Drawing on dark card
When drawing on dark card, use a light-coloured pen or pencil so that your markings are easier to see.

Balloon pump
A balloon pump is a quick and easy way of blowing up balloons. Use one and you won't run out of puff!

Outlining in pen
Outline details on your models using a black marker pen. This will emphasize the features, cover small mistakes, and make the model look neat and tidy.

HANDY TIPS

Using PVA glue

PVA glue

Poster paint

Making acrylic paint
Make your own waterproof paint by mixing poster paint with PVA glue.

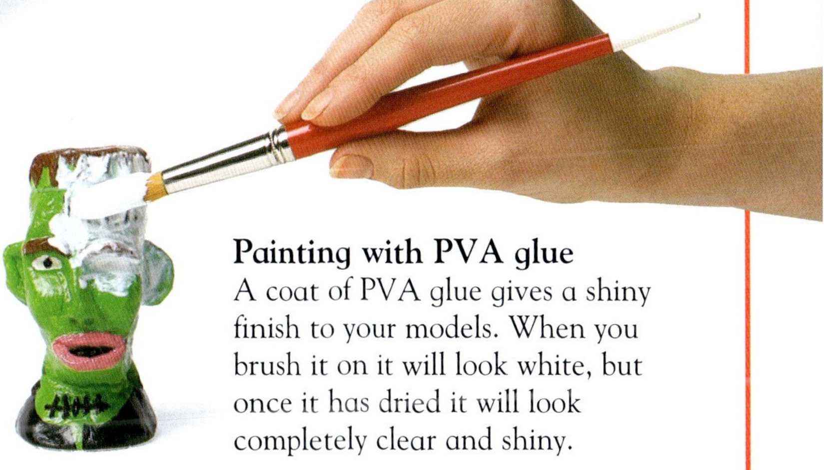

Painting with PVA glue
A coat of PVA glue gives a shiny finish to your models. When you brush it on it will look white, but once it has dried it will look completely clear and shiny.

Chalk tips

Red

Purple

Mixing pastels
Create different colours and shades by blending your chalks together using cotton wool or a paintbrush.

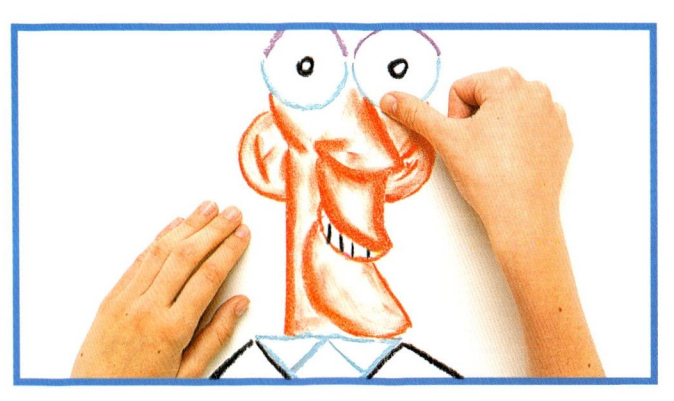

Smudging chalk
Draw a hard line in chalk. Smudge away from the line with your thumb to soften the picture.

Hanging up your Art Attacks

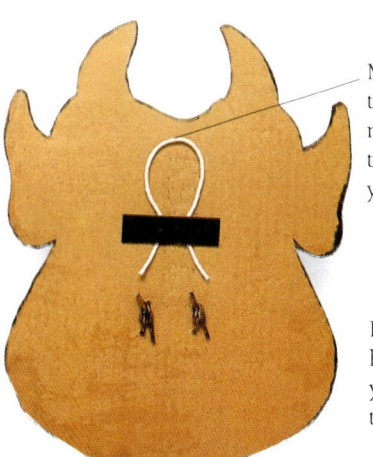

Loop the string around both of the twig ends to secure it.

Make sure the string does not show over the top of your model.

Peal the top layers off after you have stuck them down.

Hanging with a string loop
To hang light objects, such as the gargoyles, make a loop out of string and attach it with sticky tape.

Hanging with sticky tabs
To hang objects with flat surfaces, like a mirror tile, press sticky tabs firmly to each corner.

Hanging with long string
For heavier objects, such as the jungle frame, attach a long piece of string to the top corners.

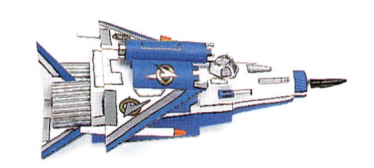

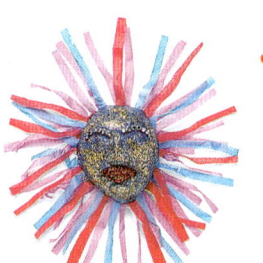

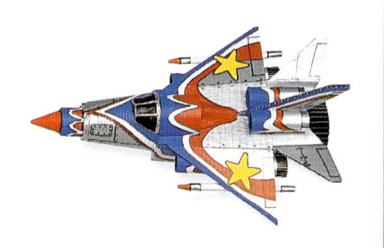

INDEX

3-D picture 28-29, 30-31, 36-37, 42-43, 44-47, 56-57

Acrylic paint 19, 20, 27, 45, 63
alien 13, 27

Balloon 34, 35, 62
balloon pump 34, 62
book cover 22-23

Calendar 6-9
card, greeting 30-31, 48-49, 51
chalk 16, 24, 25, 40, 41, 63
clingwrap 44, 45, 46, 47
coloured pencils 33, 56, 57
colour swatch 16, 17
colour wheel 17
creased art 42-43

Diary 22-23
door knocker 52-53

Fabric paint 26, 27
face 12-13, 24-25
fish 31
flower 36-37
flyer 18-21
footballer 43
footprints 14, 15
frame 10-11, 44-47, 50-51, 63
frog 31

Gargoyle 52-53, 63
geometry set 24, 25
glitter 35, 38, 39
gold pen 21, 26, 27, 60

Hand prints 14, 15

Kitchen foil 42, 43

Layer picture 28-29, 44-45
light and dark 40-41
logo 20

Magazine 50, 51
mask 34-35
mirror 50-51, 63
mobile 54-55
modelling clay 32, 33
monster 25, 53

Nail varnish 26, 27
numbers 8, 9

Paper folding 30, 31, 36, 37, 48, 54, 57
pen holder 32-33
perspective 28, 29
plastic cup 8, 19
printing 14-15
PVA glue 5, 18, 19, 33, 38, 50, 58, 59, 63

Rubbish 5, 20

Scoring 36, 37, 63
seasons 17
sequins 35
shadow 40, 41
shoe polish 23
silver pen 21, 26, 27, 45, 60
skull 11, 33, 53
skyscraper 58-61
spider 54-55
split pin 9, 12, 13, 62
stationery 14, 15
sticks 10, 11
sticky tabs 63
string 10, 11, 53, 55, 63
superman 43

Tape box 51
templates 14, 15
tissue paper 34, 35, 52
tracing paper 28, 29
T-shirt 26-27

Video cassette 58-61

Watch 6-9
waves 56-57
wiggly ears 12-13
wrapping paper 42
writing book 22